W9-AHC-497

RAVEN and the FIRST PEOPLE

Legends of the Northwest Coast

Thomas George

ESCHA
BOOKS

© 2009 by Eschia Books Inc.
First printed in 2009 10 9 8 7 6 5 4 3 2 1
Printed in Canada

All rights reserved. No part of this work covered by the copyrights hereon may be reproduced or used in any form or by any means—graphic, electronic or mechanical—without the prior written permission of the publisher, except for reviewers, who may quote brief passages. Any request for photocopying, recording, taping or storage on information retrieval systems of any part of this work shall be directed in writing to the publisher.

The Publisher: Eschia Books Inc.
Website: www.eschia.com

Library and Archives Canada Cataloguing in Publication

George, Thomas, 1977–
Raven and the first people / Thomas George.

ISBN 978-1-926696-08-9

1. Indians of North America—Northwest, Pacific—Folklore.
2. Raven (Legendary character)—Legends. I. Title.

E78.5.N77G46 2009   398.2'089970795   C2009-905708-5

Project Director: Kathy van Denderen
Editor: Nicholle Carrière
Cover Illustration: Frank Burman

PC: 1

When the people beseeched Raven for his help, he initially refused, for he did not get involved in the affairs of humans unless it affected him.

– "Raven Against the Southwest Wind"

Contents

Introduction

THERE IS A COMMON misconception when people look back to the time before the arrival of the Europeans that the tribes of the Pacific Coast apparently lived in some utopian society based on a communion between humans and nature.

Nature was certainly good to the people of the area, with abundant forests where one could find all the essentials of daily life and a bountiful sea with fish for the taking. Nature certainly gave, but it also took. Fishermen often did not come back from the catch, and hunters, if they returned, told of giant creatures of the forests and mountains. And although villages and tribes often engaged in wars over territory and internal squabbles, the people managed to carve out a decent life for themselves and were perfectly adapted for living in harmony with the conditions of their land.

With the world outside their door casting a dark shadow, the people sought comfort and tried to make sense of it all by telling stories. As night closed in and the day's tasks were put aside, the people of the longhouse would gather around the fire and tell each other fantastic tales of great floods, mythical creatures and evil spirits. They told stories of the mischievous Raven who brought light to the world, or the angry Thunderbird who flapped his wings, stomped the ground and shot light from his eyes, making the first storms, or the Great Spirit who created the world in a time before light and long before the memory of humans. But these were more than simple stories to the people of the West Coast—they were part of the fabric of daily life.

The favourite character of most of these stories was without a doubt Raven. Always out to satisfy his own needs, the Raven spirit was seen as both good and bad in Native mythology. He was a character who brought light to the world and returned the animals to the land and seas for the people to eat, but it was never done out of the goodness of his heart. Either a lustful eye or an empty stomach always motivates Raven, and any good that comes out of his adventures is usually unintended. But he is the central character in most stories, probably because his desires and his lust most often mirrored those of humans. And when it comes to the stories, Raven was simply the most entertaining for the people and I hope, dear reader, after finishing this book, you will say the same thing.

Raven Brings Light to the World

RAVEN, THE POWERFUL SPIRIT of legend, had always existed and will exist forever.

In a time long before the memory of humans, the world was a place of darkness. No light fell upon the seas or penetrated the forests. It was a time when the spirits glided through the shadows alone. For thousands of generations, they did not meet another soul in their wanderings.

Although Raven did not mind the solitude, he was beginning to tire of his own company. For Raven, not getting into any mischief was against his nature. Plus, the darkness did not make it easy to get around and, most of all, hunting for food was wearisome.

In his wanderings, Raven learned one day after a chance meeting with Tla'ik, daughter of the evil spirit Aihos, that long ago, her father had taken the light and placed it in a box that was now somewhere inside their lodge. She told Raven that her father thought the box so precious that he had hidden it so no one could easily locate it.

Raven was confident he could steal the light, but getting it would not be easy. But if there was one thing Raven was good at, it was trickery, and as he travelled the great distance to the home of Aihos, his plan to steal the light came to him.

After many days' flight, Raven finally arrived at the place where Aihos' lodge was supposed to be. However, because it was completely dark, Raven could not see exactly where the lodge was. After stumbling around in the dark for a long time, Raven's persistence paid off when he heard the voice of Aihos off in the distance.

"It is so nice that I, and I alone, possess the light. It is mine, and mine alone, to behold. I have placed it in this precious box—not even my own daughter is allowed to touch it. I shall guard the light with my life, and if anyone should come near it, they will feel my anger."

Walking in the direction that the voice was coming from, Raven finally came upon the lodge. Sitting outside, Raven waited until its inhabitant went to sleep, and then he poked and investigated every inch of the dwelling's walls looking for an opening, but he could find no door. It was obvious that Aihos wanted to protect his precious box and had used magic to disguise the entrance to his home. Groping around in the dark, Raven came across a tree and perched himself on a branch, waiting for someone to come outside.

After several days, his patience was rewarded when Aihos' daughter exited the lodge and walked to the river to fetch some water. Although he could not see her, Raven knew it was Tla'ik by the lovely melody she whistled as she made her way down to the water. Listening to her beautiful tune, Raven knew at once what he had to do.

Placing himself at the edge of the river close to where the young woman was collecting water, Raven transformed himself into the smallest of pebbles and was quickly collected up into the water jug by the girl. Thirsty after all her hard work, Tla'ik took a drink from her jug. Without her even knowing, Raven managed to slip into Tla'ik's mouth and down into her belly. Once inside, Raven moved through her system until he found a warm, comfortable spot to rest. In that spot, he transformed himself into a tiny human being. Tired at having used so much magic, Raven then fell into a deep sleep.

Tla'ik was completely unaware of the situation until a few months later, when she noticed her belly begin to swell. She did not tell her father of the changes to her body until the day that Raven finally awoke from his slumber and emerged into the world in the form of a baby boy.

At first, Aihos did not welcome the child, for his cries and need for constant attention upset the tranquility of the lodge. But with time, the infant began to soften the heart of Aihos, and the two spent much time together. Now, although Raven had taken the form of a baby, he had not forgotten his original intention. Every time Raven was left alone, he crawled about the lodge looking for the precious box that contained the light, until one day he found it hidden inside a bigger box under the bed of Aihos. Upon opening the larger box, Raven finally got a glimpse of what he had come all this way for. The evil spirit's precious box lay at the bottom of the big box, giving off faint beams of light. Aihos had taken great care to hide his treasure and had woven many magic spells to protect it from intruders, but the light was too powerful to be contained completely.

Seeing that the boy had discovered his secret, Aihos picked up the Raven child and scolded him for his curiosity. Raven knew that his plan to retrieve the light would not work in his current form and began plotting a new strategy.

During his stay in the lodge, he noticed that once a week, Tla'ik left the lodge to go down to the river to collect water. It was during her absence that Raven would have to steal the precious box.

The very next time the daughter left the lodge, Raven transformed into Tla'ik. Although Raven did not take much care in altering his appearance because Aihos could not see in the darkness, Raven did, however, make sure that his voice matched hers perfectly. Approaching Aihos now as his daughter, Raven asked in his most polite, most feminine voice, if he could see the box.

"Father, may I please hold the box in which you keep the light? I have been your trustworthy, obedient daughter as long as I can remember, and if you love me, you will let me hold your precious box."

"Now, daughter, there is nothing there for your eyes. Please do not ask," replied Aihos.

"I see you do not even trust your own daughter. Therefore, I am no longer welcome in this home. If I cannot hold the box, I will take my son and leave forever," said Raven, bending the will of a father in the way only a daughter can.

Fearing the loss of his only daughter and his new grandson, Aihos finally gave in to her demands. Raven could hardly contain his excitement as the box was placed in his hands. He brought the box within a breath of his face and gently pried the lid open. The first ray of light to escape the box fell onto Raven's face, offering its gentle warmth. As he fully opened the box, Raven saw two discs of light, one that gave off a soft, white light and one that was far brighter and shone a fiery red colour.

As the light spread over every surface of the lodge, and all that was once invisible could suddenly be seen, Aihos realized that the person standing before him was not his daughter. For although Raven could take the form of whatever he desired, he had not transformed completely because of the darkness, and when Aihos first saw his daughter, she was in human form but with the beak of a raven.

In a panic, Raven took the light in his beak, threw the box at Aihos and transformed back into his original form. Aihos tried in vain to catch Raven as he flew about the lodge. With no way to escape, Raven was in danger of losing the very thing that he had spent so much time trying to steal. But just as it seemed that all was lost, Tla'ik returned from fetching water. When she opened the door, Raven bolted for the opening and escaped the lodge with the precious light in his beak.

The moment he flew through the doorway, Raven saw the world in all its glory. From the vast fields of grass to the giant trees of the forests, and from the fast-moving rivers to the swirling oceans, the earth came to life before his eyes. The higher he flew, the more the light revealed. Best of all, Raven could see the animals and fish below. He licked his beak in anticipation of the bounty of food now before him. Raven was so taken by the sights before his eyes, he did not see that Aihos, angry at having his treasure stolen, had just thrown a rock, and it was headed straight for Raven.

Luckily, Raven turned at that very moment. It was not because he sensed any danger, but in his spiteful Raven manner, he wanted to gaze upon the defeated look of Aihos. His need to gloat over his success was what saved him from getting hit with the rock. Raven moved at the last second, but in his haste to avoid the stone, he dropped the soft, white disc of light.

Down to the earth the disc tumbled. Raven dove after it, but it was too late. The light hit the ground and smashed into a million pieces that flew up into the sky. Raven looked up to see that the pieces of light remained floating in the heavens, and the largest of the pieces had become the moon.

Now that he was finally able to look over the land, Raven's thoughts turned to hunger. He could see all the food beneath him, but with the remaining disc of light in his beak, he could not eat. This was a problem for Raven, because he loved to eat.

To solve his dilemma, he threw the bright, fiery red disc into the air, where it settled on the horizon and became the sun.

As Raven searched for food on the shores of the ocean in the light of day, Aihos was back at his lodge, rambling on in anger at having lost his precious box. But all was not lost, for Aihos saw his daughter for the first time, and she was as beautiful as the setting sun.

The Young Woman and the Great Flood

In ancient times, the land was covered in massive forests in which, from ages long past, dwelt the spirits. It was a time when humans and beasts lived in harmony, but as time passed, humans began to destroy the great forests. Giant forest spirits, all descendants of the Great Spirit, took an oath to protect the remaining forests without regard for their lives, even if it meant warring with the humans.

ALONG THE SHORES OF distant waters lived the tribe of the great chief, Ka'temot. His people were the most prosperous in all the known lands, and as the population grew, the village needed more and more raw materials. At first, the people of the village only took what they needed from the land, but soon greed began to settle in their hearts, and the earth around the village began to die.

The people needed the trees of the forest to build homes, and they dug deep into the mountains to get metal for weapons. They turned what was once a lush, green land into a brown, lifeless plain. But humankind's greed knows no bounds, and the village sent workers farther and farther away to cut down more trees and to dig up more earth. When Chief Ka'temot looked out from behind the village walls into the surrounding lands, he did not see destruction—he saw power, and he wanted more for his people. But he knew the spirits would not give up without a fight, and Chief Ka'temot was ready for war.

Despite his wicked ways towards the natural world, the spirits blessed Chief Ka'temot and his wife with a beautiful baby girl. The couple loved their little daughter with all their hearts and took her everywhere they went. The girl even softened the chief's lust for power, and he began spending more and more time with his child. When they had time, the new family's favourite pastime was fishing together on a nearby river.

One afternoon, while the chief brought in the fish, his wife sat on the shore cleaning and gutting the catch. Their daughter sat in a basket at her mother's side and watched. Suddenly, a storm whipped down off the mountains and blew the basket containing the child into the fast-moving water. Her father jumped in to try to save her, but the spirit of the river, who had heard of the chief's crimes against the forest, kept pushing him away, and Chief Ka'temot could only watch as his daughter disappeared down the river.

The basket with the little girl floated downriver and eventually out to sea. For days, the basket drifted on the water until it finally landed on the shores of the land of the Wolf tribe, where the human child was found by a young cub and brought to the chief.

The tribe was led by the great white She-Wolf, who for thousands of years had guarded her forests from destruction. She was a wise and honourable chief, but her hatred for humans exceeded her compassion. Just as the She-Wolf was about to bite the child's head off, she happened to look into the little girl's eyes. But instead of seeing the eyes of a human, she saw those of a Wolf. In all her years, she had never seen something so out of the ordinary. The She-Wolf then decreed to her people and all the spirits that although the infant was human in appearance, she was a member of the Wolf tribe in her heart.

The little girl was adopted into the Wolf tribe and raised by the She-Wolf herself. She grew up never knowing who her parents were and, from a very early age, learned a deep hatred towards the human race.

Without his daughter to calm his lust for power, Chief Ka'temot continued to build his army and expand his kingdom. The spirits took his child, they blackened his heart to the suffering of the world. Farther and farther into the forest he pressed in search of more materials with which to build his kingdom, and with each step, he came closer to war with the guardian spirits of the woods.

Looking out across his kingdom, Chief Ka'temot said to his wife, "For generations, our people have wasted their time praying to these spirits when the spirits have done nothing for them. You see before you all that I have done for my village. I have provided food, water and shelter for thousands of people, and the spirits repay my good deeds by taking my child. Gone are the days when we prayed to the Great Spirit of the forest. We look ahead to the future now, and progress is our religion. I vow before you, my wife, that I will kill the Great Spirit and keep his head as my trophy. If I have to chop down every tree until the Great Spirit reveals himself, I will. The spirit guardians are proud, and I will make war with them and force the Great Spirit to reveal himself."

As the chief prepared his army for war, so did the spirit guardians of the forest, led by the Bear chief, Kakeiq. Chief Kakeiq was a proud and noble beast who had served the Great Spirit for thousands of years. He held dominion over the Bear tribe and the greatest part of the forest, and he had kept the peace for generations, but because of Chief Ka'temot's hunger for power, he knew there would be no option but war.

To discuss the plan for war, Chief Kakeiq called together a council of the elder guardians. The chiefs of the Eagle, Beaver, Mink and Wolf clans travelled many days to arrive in the land of the Bears.

"I have called you here, brothers and sisters, because we have been left with no options," said Chief Kakeiq. "That power-hungry Chief Ka'temot has forced our hand to war, and we must unite and destroy the humans. Once they lived in peace with us, but they have been corrupted."

"Wise guardian of the Bear tribe," said the She-Wolf. "I, too, feel your hatred for the humans. Long have we battled them, and many of our people have we lost, but I do not see why we must send all our people to be slaughtered. For if we lose this war, we lose everything. I have brought along my daughter, but fear not and do not slay her, for she is no human. Look into her eyes, and you will see the soul of a Wolf."

"Chief of the Wolves, you have fought courageously for many generations, but your words are foolish, and now you come before us with this filthy human creature," said Chief Kakeiq.

"I have brought her here before the council to show you that not all the humans are lost. She came to us and I almost killed her, but in her eyes I saw the soul of a Wolf. The Great Spirit, in his wisdom, placed her in my care for a reason. Wiping out the humans is not the answer. No good shall come of it. If we were to return her to her people, maybe we could stop the war," said the She-Wolf.

Some of the other chiefs began to agree with the words of the She-Wolf, but then Chief Kakeiq spoke. "We all have seen what the humans are capable of. The Great Spirit is in danger, and no child will save us now. The forests get smaller and smaller by the day. The humans have forsaken the Great Spirit, and their lust for power will not end. If we do not unite and stop them now, we will lose everything."

The other chiefs cheered the words of Chief Kakeiq, all but the She-Wolf. She could see the chosen path leading to nothing but death and destruction. The She-Wolf had hoped that her daughter would be able to bring peace to the two worlds, but rage had taken root in the hearts of the guardian spirits and war would soon follow.

Many years passed as the two sides built up their armies, and the girl grew into a beautiful young woman. When she was old enough, she began to see the difference between herself and the Wolf tribe and started to question where she had come from.

"Mother, why do I not look like you and your people?" asked the young girl. "In my heart I feel like a Wolf, but I look like a human."

"Daughter, I have kept your secret for far too long," said the She-Wolf. "You came to me many years ago, and I thought you were a normal human. I was going to kill you, but when I saw your eyes, I could tell you had the soul of a Wolf. I knew the Great Spirit sent you to me for a reason, so I raised you as one of my own. Your real parents are those who have been destroying the forest."

The sudden revelation shocked the young woman and sent her into a deep depression. So many questions ran through her head. Why was she not like other humans? Why was she not like her Wolf mother? Why were her birth parents so intent on destroying the forests and the spirits that lived within them? For days, she wandered through the woods pondering all these questions, until she came to a place of great enchantment and beauty.

Sunlight broke through the thick canopy of trees and illuminated the clearest pond she had ever seen. Great trees dotted the pond like islands, and in the centre stood the largest tree of all. In the distance, through the trees, she could see a figure moving slowly towards her. It was difficult to see clearly through the trees and the shadows, but the figure looked like a deer or elk, with a glorious crown of horns atop its head. Slowly, the figure moved into the light, and the young girl could see that although the creature had the body of an elk, its face was flat and looked more like that of a human. In each of its footsteps, up would spring the most beautiful grass and flowers, but then they would immediately wither and die. It was then that she knew she was in the presence of the Great Spirit, for it gives life but can also take it away.

She watched as the Great Spirit approached the pond and took one step towards her. Her eyes widened as the spirit stepped onto the water as if it were dry land. With measured steps, the Great Spirit kept its huge eyes directly on the young woman and walked straight towards her. Falling to her knees, she bowed her head. There were so many questions she wanted to ask and so many answers she wanted to hear. She wanted to tell the Great Spirit of the coming war and of the humans' destruction of the forests, but she could not move her tongue.

Stepping off the water and standing before the young woman, the Great Spirit smiled at her and stared deep into her eyes. She tried to fix her gaze somewhere else, but she could not look away. The girl suddenly became tired, and her eyes fell shut. She could hear nothing save for the breathing of the Great Spirit before her, and then it spoke.

"Child, fear not what the future holds. You have so many questions as to why you are of both worlds. But I have placed you here for a reason, and that reason shall be revealed to you. Do not give in to hatred; if you do, you will be corrupted," said the Great Spirit.

When the young woman opened her eyes, the Great Spirit was gone. She ran back to her home and told her mother what she had seen.

"I believe this to be an omen of good fortune. We must go at once and tell the chief of the Bears not to make war," said the She-Wolf.

The girl jumped on her mother's back, and they sped through the forest to the land of the Bear clan, but it was already too late. The Bears had moved their army out to battle the humans.

Wave after wave of Bears led the charge upon the humans' village. But the humans were prepared and fired so many arrows into the sky that they blocked out the sun. The Bears put up a valiant fight, but the day belonged to the humans. The great warrior Chief Kakeiq was mortally injured in the battle and commanded his warriors to retreat. Chief Ka'temot watched the battle from afar and was pleased at how it had unfolded.

"We have won the day, but the Great Spirit of the forest still lives. Gather some of the skins of the Bears and cover yourselves with them. Go to the injured Bear chief. He will think you are his people returned from the land of the dead, and he will lead us directly to the Great Spirit," said Chief Ka'temot. "I will follow close behind, and once he has led us to the Great Spirit, I will use my arrows to slice its head off."

Chief Ka'temot sent out his best warriors, who skinned the dead Bears and put on their coats. Moving through the forest as though they were Bears, Chief Ka'temot's warriors found the injured Bear chief, who lay upon the ground, blinded by two arrows stuck in his eyes. Although he could not see, the chief could smell that his warriors had returned.

"My children, you have returned from the land of the dead. We must go to the Great Spirit. He will heal us so the battle can continue. We will be renewed, my brothers!" shouted the bloodied chief. "Although I am blind, I see more clearly now than ever. Come, for our victory is at hand."

Overcome by rage and pride, Chief Kakeiq of the Bears ran through the forest towards the land where the Great Spirit dwelt. Although blind and bleeding, the stubborn Bear knocked over trees and broke rocks as he made his way through the woods. He was nearly at his destination when the She-Wolf and her daughter stopped him and pleaded for his understanding.

"Great Chief Kakeiq, please stop what you are doing. You do not understand," said the young woman. "Your pride has kept you from seeing that you have lost the war. These are not your children. They are humans in disguise."

"No! I can taste their defeat. I know the Great Spirit will restore us and we will destroy the human scum. Why should I listen to a half-human, half-wolf girl? Onward, brothers, to the land of the Great Spirit and victory!"

"Chief Kakeiq is too stubborn and full of pride to stop now," said the She-Wolf. "His heart has been corrupted. There is no way to halt what has been set in motion."

Chief Kakeiq pushed through the forest and finally came to the home of the Great Spirit. The young woman had tried to reason with him, but the darkness of hatred had blackened his heart.

Breaking through the trees, the Bear chief and his impostor army stopped before the sacred pond, closely followed by the She-Wolf and her daughter. Hidden in the woods was the young woman's real father, Chief Ka'temot.

Everyone was silent as they gazed upon the beauty of the sacred forest home of the Great Spirit. The young woman broke the silence and continued to plead with the Bear chief to return to his home, but her words were useless as he was too consumed with hatred to listen.

"Great Spirit, heed my call. Save us from destruction!" shouted the Bear chief, releasing a proud war cry that nearly deafened everyone.

Chief Ka'temot knew that the time was at hand and readied his arrow. "All right, men," he whispered. "Be prepared, for when I remove the head of the Great Spirit, we must flee swiftly."

"The Great Spirit! He approaches!" said the Bear chief, smelling the air with his giant nose.

The Great Spirit appeared out of the shadows of the forest, still in the form of an elk. A hush befell everyone surrounding the pond as the Great Spirit took its first steps out into the light. Its large eyes and angelic face stared directly at the young woman as he moved silently towards them, the sound of his footfalls echoing through the forest. The Great Spirit walked across the water and stood before the Bear chief. Without a word, it blew a gentle breath on the Bear and he died.

Chief Ka'temot watched from a distance and readied his arrow. Staring directly at his target, he wondered to himself if he was making the right choice. But then he remembered the pain of losing his only daughter.

"Watch carefully, gentlemen. I am going to show you how to kill a god," said Chief Ka'temot, releasing the arrow.

Flying through the air with tremendous velocity, the arrow struck the Great Spirit in the neck and came out the other side. A large hole began to form. The Great Spirit's body appeared not to be made of blood and bone, but of a liquid that was as dark as the night sky and filled with stars. Chief Ka'temot released a second arrow, and the Great Spirit's head came off with a pop.

As soon as the head hit the ground, the chief and his men sprang from their hiding places and placed it in a box.

"You fool," said the young woman. "Your hatred has blinded you. Can you not see that your daughter stands before you?"

Chief Ka'temot looked upon the young woman and recognized her as his own. "I have been a fool," he said, with tears running down his face. "My pride and ambition have doomed us all."

The body of the Great Spirit did not lie still on the ground, but instead began to change. The form of the elk disappeared, transforming into a giant taller than the trees, its body made of liquid sky. It grew and grew, but had no head with which to guide itself.

"We must return the head. That is the only way to appease the spirit," the young woman cried. She grabbed the box and jumped onto the She-Wolf's back. They ran to the nearest mountaintop and held the head up to the sky.

A great wind swept through the forest as the Great Spirit's body wandered in search of its head.

"O, Great Spirit," cried the young woman from atop the mountain, "forgive us. I offer you back your head. Reclaim it so that you can restore peace and balance to the world."

The Great Spirit could sense her cries and wandered through the forest towards her. She held onto the head firmly as the Great Spirit's headless body approached. With its long arms, it reached out and grabbed the head from the girl and returned it to the top of its body.

But the Great Spirit did not return to its elk form. Rather, once its head was attached, it suddenly began to swell. Its liquid body grew to such an incredible size that it nearly blocked out the sun, and then all at once it burst, sending out a wall of water that swept across the land. Chief Ka'temot and his village were swept away, all the signs of war disappeared, and all the conflict came to an end. The flood wiped out all humanity, and when the waters receded, only one person remained.

Looking out across the world from the top of the mountain, the young woman could see that where the forests had been destroyed, the Great Spirit brought back life. And where there had been only war, peace reigned throughout the lands.

From the sky, the young woman suddenly heard the voice of the Great Spirit.

"You were made for great things. You will provide guidance for the new human race that is to come. But you shall not return to the land as you once were. From now on, you will be part of the spirit world and will always be known as Mother Earth."

Mighty White Raven

WHEN THE TSIMSHIAN PEOPLE returned to their homes after the Great Flood, they discovered that all the animals had mysteriously disappeared. They knew the animals had survived because, like the Tsimshian, they had fled into the high mountains and avoided getting swept away, but upon the return of the Tsimshian to their ancestral lands, none of the animals had come back. After a few weeks and still no sign of the creatures of the forests, skies and mountains, the Tsimshian people began to worry. Without the animals, they would have no food to eat and no clothes to wear.

In order to find out what had happened to all the animals, the shaman was summoned and asked to call for the help of the powerful White Raven.

"Great White Raven, come to the assistance of your people and find our animals. They have no doubt disappeared by the will of some evil spirit. We beseech you, White Raven, in our time of great desperation. Aid us, and we shall erect many totems in your honour and celebrate your name in tale and legend for generations."

Hearing the pleas of the Tsimshian people, White Raven took to the skies to survey the lands to see if what they said was true. High into the skies White Raven flew. Passing over the great seas he could see no fish in the waters, over the mountain ranges he saw no movement, and down in the valleys he could see no signs of life. He flapped his mighty wings and flew to the flatlands of the east and the cold grounds to the north and still nothing stirred below.

Turning back to report to the Tsimshian people what he had seen, his keen eyes spotted the smoke from a cabin along the shores of a lake. Outside the cabin, he spotted an old woman chopping wood for her fireplace. White Raven at once knew this to be the home of a very powerful evil spirit. He flew closer to the cabin, out of the old woman's line of sight, and could hear the sound of all the missing animals somewhere inside the cabin's walls.

"I have found the missing beasts," White Raven said to himself. "Now I must use my magic powers to defeat the evil spirit. But I must be careful—if I use all my magic to overcome her, I will not have enough left to free the animals. I must use my keen intelligence to defeat her and somehow get her away from the cabin."

Perching high in a tree, White Raven thought for several days until he came up with a plan that would not fail.

Transforming himself into human form dressed in the attire of a Tsimshian hunter, White Raven emerged from the forest and knocked on the door of the old woman's cabin.

At first there was only silence, but when White Raven pounded on the door once more, he heard a voice from inside.

"Go away!" said the old spirit.

"Please, good lady of the woods, I am in need of a warm fire," said White Raven.

"You are not welcome here. Leave before you regret knocking on my door."

White Raven did not pay her any attention and continued to plead through the door. "My lady, I am but a weary hunter who has been travelling the forest for several days. I have killed a goat and two large elk from a herd on the other side of that ridge just beyond the lake. I beg of you, I need a place to rest before bringing my kill back to the village and my people."

Of course, White Raven knew this was not true, but he understood the greed of the old woman perfectly well and knew that word of an elk herd would pique her curiosity.

Opening the door, the old lady stuck her head out and looked over her visitor with her evil, clouded eyes.

"You're a liar! This cannot be, for I alone possess all the animals of the world."

"But you are wrong. I killed three animals just yesterday, and there are many more for your collection," said White Raven. "Why, I even saw some bears, but they were too far away for my arrows."

"I do not trust you, stranger, but I wish to see these herds of animals for myself. You must show me the way."

White Raven tried to convince the old hag that he was too tired from the day's hunt to lead her, but she would not leave her prize possessions in the hands of a stranger. Reluctantly, White Raven left the cabin and headed out into the woods with the old lady. Coming out of the woods on the edge of the lake, White Raven pointed ahead to where he said he had seen the animals. The old woman stood at the edge of the water, straining her eyes to see where the beasts were hidden. Seizing the opportunity, White Raven pushed her into the lake. As she struggled to free herself from the cold water, White Raven changed into his bird form and flew at full speed back to the cabin.

Once inside, he found the animals locked in a cage at the rear of cabin and used his powerful beak to break the lock. Out poured the animals—deer, bears, elk, squirrels, porcupines and more broke for the safety of the forest. Finally, all the animals had escaped from the cabin except for the snake.

Long ago, the snake was not the same animal we know today. Back then, he did not crawl on his belly, and his temperament was calm. That is why he remained behind and slowly made his way out of the cabin, stopping to take a sip of water from a puddle and stretch in the midday sun. White Raven tried to move the snake along faster, but the lazy creature ignored his pleas.

It was too late, anyway. The old woman had returned and was in a foul mood. When she saw that the snake was her only remaining pet, she ran forward and scooped him up in her hands. But the normally calm snake bit the old woman's hand, forcing her to drop him to the ground.

"If you wish to leave, snake, then go!" she screamed. "But you will be cursed forever for your insolence. From this moment on, you will forever be forced to crawl on your belly and your legendary calmness will be replaced by the most vile and hateful attitude. Neither human nor animal will call you friend."

The old woman waved her hand, and at once the snake fell to the ground on his belly, and when White Raven rushed to his aid, the snake tried to bite him. That is why snakes now crawl on their bellies and are so quick to strike out.

With all her pets gone, the old woman turned to White Raven.

"You, White Raven, have done me the most harm of all," she said pointing at him. "You know of the laws that say no spirit shall lie to another, and you, White Raven, have told a multitude of lies."

Knowing that she could not kill him, White Raven simply laughed at the old hag for making such claims.

"Spare me your sanctimony, old crone," mocked White Raven. "You have been beaten by the best. Return to your lodge to lick your wounds, and never bother the creatures again."

But the old woman did not heed White Raven's wishes and sat down upon the ground. She began to move her mouth, though no words came out. Then she raised her eyes, which had turned completely white, to the heavens and began chanting out loud. Although there was no wind before, suddenly a powerful gust smashed into White Raven, almost knocking him off his feet. Dark clouds began to form, and the air became thick and humid. The old woman sprang to her feet and pointed directly at White Raven.

"You have broken the law of the Great Spirit, and you shall be punished for your transgressions. You are bathed in the brilliant white feathers of heaven, but from now on, you will be forced to wear a coat of black plumes as evidence of your lies. Since time began, you were a trusted spirit, but from now on, you will bear the mark of the pretender."

With those finals words, a bolt of lightning descended from the sky, directly striking White Raven. In a flash of light and smoke, his coat changed from brilliant white to coal black.

When the smoke had cleared, the old woman simply got up and returned to her cabin without another word.

Raven found that without his coat of white feathers, he had lost some of his magical powers, and the spirits, animals and humans of the world no longer paid him the same reverence as before. But as they had promised, the Tsimshian people erected many great totem poles depicting the sacrifice that Raven made in his battle with the old woman and the return of the animals of the land, sea and air.

Raven Versus the Spider

There was no doubt among the people of the land that Raven was indeed an annoyance to humankind, but a service rendered to humans long ago made people tolerate his presence for all time.

BACK IN THE TIME before the memory of living people, there existed a world in which humans and spirits both walked the earth. It was a time of plenty as well as a time of great fear for humankind, for although the spirits of this world could be generous, they could also be cruel.

One of the most loathsome of the spirits dwelt deep in the mountains on the mainland and took the form of a hideous spider. It was so great in size that the very ground it walked on trembled, and all the animals of the forests scurried out of its way to avoid certain death. The spider was covered with long, spine-like hairs, each as sharp as an arrow, and it had numerous eyes that all stared with a glassy blackness. The creature's whole body was as dark as night except for a small patch of red on its back, and every time it opened its venom-filled mouth, poisonous gases crept forth and destroyed every living thing in its path.

The people who had the misfortune to dwell on the mainland were in constant fear of the spider and were forced to pay the spirit a weekly homage in the form of food. If a village failed to pay its respects to the creature, the spider would descend from the mountains and lay waste to the villagers' homes and farms. To slake its great thirst, the spider had been drinking up all the fresh water that poured out of the mountains, leaving the rivers and streams below completely dry. The villages were in dire straits, and without rivers to supply water and fish, the people were on the verge of death.

The chiefs of the villages held council and decided to put an end to the evil spirit's tyranny. They sent out over one hundred of their best warriors to slay the beast, but only one man returned. He was covered in blood and his hair had turned completely white. The chiefs all crowded around the man to learn what had happened to the rest of the warriors, but the horror he had witnessed left him without speech or reason. These were indeed dark times for the people of the mainland.

In desperation, the council of chiefs sent a small group of delegates into far-off lands to look for someone to help them defeat the spider. For many moons, the men from the doomed tribes walked through the ancients forests of the mainland and crossed deadly mountain trails, but they could find no tribe willing to help their cause despite their warnings that once the spider had finished off their tribes, he would surely make his way to them. With only one day's supplies left and with hope fading among the delegates, they came upon the home of Raven.

Raven, who was living in the form of a human and going by the name of Ta'qliki, greeted the sorrowful group.

"O, why does such sadness fill the air around you? What tribe has done you such harm?" Ta'qliki asked them as they approached his lodge.

"Brother, we have come to seek your assistance. Our villages have been under the tyranny of the evil spider spirit of the mountains. He has killed all our best warriors, and his unquenchable thirst has dried up all the waters. Please listen to our story and grant us your assistance, or I am afraid we will all perish."

Ta'qliki listened intently as the men told the story of the spider of the mountains and how for many months he had terrorized the people of the mainland. They told how they had sent more than one hundred well-armed warriors to do battle, but only one shell of a man returned. They told how the spider's insatiable hunger and thirst had ravaged the lands of all the animals they hunted and had dried up the rivers so that the salmon visited no more. They warned Ta'qliki that if he did not help, their fate would eventually fall on his doorstep.

Ta'qliki felt great sorrow for the people of the mainland but was more concerned with the matter of the spider coming to him. It was very uncommon for Ta'qliki to meddle in the affairs of humans, but the threat of losing his favourite meal of salmon was enough for him to promise to assist them with their problem. Ta'qliki was only interested in helping others if his actions also helped himself.

"Come inside and rest your weary heads for a few days while I think up a plan to rid you of this spider," Ta'qliki said. Inside the lodge, the men found a generous supply of salmon, dried clams, berries and other delights already laid out for them, which they ate with zeal. After eating, the men laid down and fell into the deepest of slumbers.

While the men slept, Ta'qliki transformed himself back into Raven and took to the skies, flying for three days. He travelled to the land of his visitors to see for himself the damage that the spider had done. At first, everything appeared normal, but soaring over a ridge, he came upon a sight he had never seen before. Whole forests laid bare, the air smelling of death and the once-forceful rivers reduced to a pathetic trickle. There were no animals to hunt and no fish in the waters. This truly was a land devoid of life.

Using his incredible vision, Raven spotted the white, bleached bones of the many warriors who had lost their lives trying to dispose of the mighty spider. The sight of the bones of so many brave men strewn about made Raven's feathers shake, and he climbed higher into the air to escape the stench of death. Up high, he could see that the entire range of mountains had been drained of life, and at the eastern end of the valley, he spotted the cavern where the spider dwelt. It was there that he finally saw the beast, with its bloated, black abdomen, its eight, tree-sized legs and the black, uncaring eyes of a true demon. Flying high above so as not to alert the monster to his presence, Raven took one more look at the challenge that lay before him, and then returned to his lodge.

The men were waiting for Raven, who emerged from the forest in his human form as Ta'qliki.

"My friends, because the spider endangers not only your lives but my way of life as well, I will assist you."

Leaving the men to return to their villages on their own, Ta'qliki ate a hearty meal of salmon, then once again transformed into Raven and took to the winds for his journey to the land of the spider. Up he flew over emerald green seas, the mighty coastal forests and the snow-capped mountains to the east. Raven knew he was getting closer to the lair of the spider, for the air took on a horrible stench, the trees that once stood mighty and tall lay rotting on the forest floor, and no water flowed down the slopes into the valley. Off in the distance, he could see that the giant spider lay sleeping in the sun, no doubt having consumed some poor, unfortunate soul and quenched his thirst at the source of the valley's rivers. Seeing that the beast was fast asleep, Raven set about putting his plan into action.

Just beyond the lair of the spider, Raven found a narrow passageway that would serve him well. His plan was to lure the giant into an area where he could not easily manoeuvre and get the best of the beast. But first, he had to gain its attention.

Taking a large rock in his beak, Raven flew up high, directly above the sleeping spider. Aiming carefully, he let the stone fall towards its intended target. When the stone struck the fattened body of the beast, it awoke with a terrible scream and immediately looked about for the perpetrator. The cold, black eyes of the spider scanned the valley high and low, until its gaze fell upon Raven, who was perched on a rock near the narrow passageway. Seeing the great spider up close with its rancid breath and dripping fangs made Raven shiver, but if this was to be a battle of wits, Raven held a distinct advantage.

"Great slayer of men and beasts, you have reigned supreme over this land and I come to pay you the homage you so rightly deserve."

Not trusting the stranger, the spider moved in closer to get a better look at its visitor.

"I have come from a far-off land to honour you with a feast like you have never seen before. You just have to follow me and the prize shall be yours," urged Raven.

Raven knew he had won the spider's confidence as its mouth began to water at the prospect of the feast.

With each step he took closer to the spider, Raven could smell the putrid breath of the beast and knew that if he did not move quickly, he would become its next meal. Darting through the narrow passage-way and hiding beneath a pile of rocks, he watched as the spider slowly approached. But the spider had not survived for so many years without having some sense in its head, and just before entering the passageway, the creature stopped and looked around.

Realizing that his plan might fall apart, Raven employed his legendary wit to get the spider through the narrow opening.

"Oh, great spider spirit. I have spent many days gathering all sorts of delectable treasures from far-away lands for your pleasure. But I could only carry them to this spot, for I am just a bird and my wings are weak," said Raven.

To ensure that the spider walked into his trap, Raven had placed several large salmon on planks of wood in the centre of the passageway.

At the sight and smell of the fresh fish, the spider lost all worries of an ambush and headed straight for the bait. But just before it could close its jaws on the salmon, the spider's engorged abdomen became wedged between the walls of the passageway, and despite thrashing mightily, it could not move.

Exiting from behind his pile of rocks, Raven looked over at the giant spider and stood triumphantly in front of his enemy. "Slayer of women and children, destroyer of forests and rivers, your reign of terror is at an end. The people of the villages below have suffered long enough at your hands, and your evil will not spread to other lands."

Moving around to the large abdomen of the giant spider, Raven thrust his pointed beak into its flesh. From the wound came a powerful torrent of water that rushed out of the passageway, down the mountainside and into the dried-up rivers and streams.

As the water continued to gush forth from the spider's abdomen, the creature began to shrink. In a matter of minutes, the spider was no bigger than a hummingbird. Raven looked out across the valley and saw that as the waters returned, the fish, which had been sleeping in the mud, emerged and began to swim again. Seeds began sprouting all across the valley, and the animals of the forests returned. Raven was proud of what he had done.

The spider, which lay shrivelled in the mud, looked up at Raven. "Great Raven, you have outwitted me and taken away my power. But I am not defeated. Although I cannot feast on the bodies of humans in my current form, be warned that I will always be around, looking for my next meal to grow fat on. I will lurk in corners, under rocks and in the trees, feeding and growing, until one day, I will return and have my vengeance on this land."

Raven looked down upon the tiny, defeated spider and laughed.

"Try all you want, evil spirit, but my powers are far greater than yours. The hole in your body will remain forever, and your children's children will also be afflicted with this mark. However, I am not cruel. From this hole, you will be able to spin the most intricate of webs to ensnare your dinner, but this mark will ensure that you can never grow to your once-horrible size. It is my gift and my curse to you."

With that, Raven took to the skies and returned to his lodge to satisfy the hunger he had worked up in defeating the spider.

Raven and the Clam

LONG AFTER THE WATERS of the Great Flood had receded and life was once again as it had been, Raven walked the beaches of the coast looking for a meal that might have washed up on shore.

As his feet crushed the sand below, his all-seeing black eyes scanned the beach for tasty morsels of food to satisfy his hunger. The sun was just beginning to rise over the mountains to the east, and Raven paused to look upon the gift that he had brought to the world. A glittering ray of light burst over the tops of the mountains and illuminated the entire coastline. But Raven found all the beauty boring, for there was no one to share it with. Releasing a great sigh, Raven took to the sky to continue hunting for his morning meal. He prayed with all his heart to the Great Spirit to send him something to break the boredom.

"Caw, caw. Is anyone there?" Raven called mockingly out to the empty lands. Expecting to hear nothing, Raven was astounded when he heard a faint noise—something that sounded like a thousand muffled voices.

Scanning the beaches below, his eyes fell upon a giant clam rolling about in the surf. Raven had never seen anything like it before and landed on the beach to get a closer look. Pulling the clam from the reach of the waves with his powerful beak, he now could clearly hear that sounds were coming from inside the clam's shell.

Using his talons to pry apart the shell, Raven could see a multitude of tiny creatures cowering away from the light of an unknown world. Although Raven did not know what they were, he knew that playing with them would ease his boredom for the moment. But the creatures would not come out. He tried shaking them out, but they held on firmly. The sight of the vast new lands outside their home and, of course, the menacing black figure of Raven must have been frightening for the little creatures.

Raven had an idea. Tilting his head down to the clam, he peered in and began to gently talk to the creatures. At first they ran from him, but soon Raven's magical tongue persuaded one of them to come into the light and leave its old world behind.

The bravest of the creatures stepped out into the light of the world. Raven could see that the creatures walked on two legs like himself but that they had no feathers and no hair, except for a small patch on the top of their heads. Their arms were tiny, and they had no beaks to use to open shells. Raven truly did find them to be strange. Then Raven remember he had heard tales of a time before the Great Flood when these creatures called humans walked the earth, but their memory and history had been washed away from the world by the floodwaters.

Slowly, the new people of the earth ventured out of the shell—they were the first Haida people.

Raven watched the curious creatures as they explored their new surroundings. He laughed when he saw one of them stumble around or especially when one of them tried to catch an elk for dinner with no weapon. Raven taught the people a few techniques for survival, but after some time, he became bored with the new creatures. Suddenly, he realized why, for all the humans shared a common appendage—they were all men. Raven looked through the entire population and found no women among them. How was this new species to entertain Raven if they had no female kind?

The last place he thought to look was inside the mouth of the clam. Parting the edges of the hard outer shell, Raven peered into the clam's warm, wet mouth. He pushed aside the soft flesh with a finger but could not find what he was looking for. It was at that moment that a devious thought entered his mind. Taking the strongest man from the bunch, Raven placed the mouth of the clam below the man's belly. In a rush of feelings and sensations, the man released his energy into the clam and then they all fell into a deep sleep.

The clam closed its mouth and dug itself deep into the sand. On the next full moon, the clam emerged from the sand and opened its shell to the night sky. From the mouth of the clam came a thousand beautiful, long-haired women. Stumbling onto the beach and talking animatedly among themselves, the women made such a racket that they woke the men and Raven from their deep slumber. The Raven watched as each of the men gathered up one of the women for his own, and they spread out across the lands where they prospered in peace.

Raven was happy at the strange turn of events that had just taken place, for he would now always have someone to break the boredom.

Raven Against the Southwest Wind

―――≈≈≈≈≈≈≈―――

THE SPIRIT OF THE SOUTHWEST WIND was a temperamental being that had no respect for life, be it human, animal or even plant life. For days on end, he battered the people of the coast with his fury, causing damage to people's homes and uprooting the mightiest of trees. The people pleaded with the Southwest Wind to go away, for he had already overstayed his welcome on the coast. However, the more they pleaded, the more furiously he lashed out. The wind had picked up to such a speed that it was impossible for the people to go out in their canoes to fish. When the people beseeched Raven for his help, he initially refused, for he did not get involved in the affairs of humans unless it affected him. Only when the stocks of dried salmon ran out did Raven hear their calls for help.

Annoyed with the lack of food and the constant noise, Raven decided that he would save the people from the tyranny of the Southwest Wind.

Luckily, the Southwest Wind was not active all the time, and one night, the spirit calmed his fury and retired to his home on an island in faraway waters. Raven then set out on the long journey to the home of the Southwest Wind in order to reason with the ancient spirit. For many days, Raven travelled over the waters to the southwest before coming upon the desolate island home of the wind spirit.

"Spirit of the Southwest Wind, calm your tempestuous anger," Raven cried out.

Hearing that he had a visitor, the Southwest Wind opened the door to his lodge with a strong gust of air that carried his voice to Raven's ear. "Leave this place at once," he whispered, and with another violent gust of wind, he blew Raven back to the coast, where the bird could not bother him any longer.

This lack of respect angered Raven greatly, and he called in his cousins, the birds, for their assistance. "Great cousins of mine," Raven called out. "I need your help in besting the Southwest Wind. He has become a nuisance to the coastal tribes and has made it nearly impossible for us to take flight. We must take back the skies from this malicious spirit."

"We hear your call, great Raven," called out the clan of the Eagle.

"We will heed your words," called out the clan of the Crow. "But how can we birds combat such a powerful spirit?"

"Do not doubt yourselves, brothers," said Raven. "We might be small, but we are wise. We shall use the combined power of our wings to blow the wind to the lands at the edge of the oceans."

So all the birds gathered in the sky, aimed their wings and waited for the arrival of the Southwest Wind. Raven had called so many of the bird clans together that they nearly blocked out the sun. The birds did not have to wait long for their nemesis to arrive. With the coming of the morning sun, the Southwest Wind announced his return to the coast with a sudden gust that nearly knocked the birds from the sky. But the feathered clans held strong and began beating their wings as fast as they could. Combined, they whipped up a typhoon-force gale that gave the Southwest Wind pause, but the ancient spirit returned with a gust that knocked the birds up against the mountains. Having won the battle, the Southwest Wind smashed into the coast with a horrible fury that for lasted three days. His wrath sent all the animals and people running for safety within the walls of the mountains. Raven had lost the battle, but he did not give up easily.

After the Southwest Wind's fury died down and the spirit returned once more to his home, Raven set about making another plan to get rid of the spirit.

Walking down to the ocean, Raven called upon the creatures of the sea to help banish the wind spirit. Summoning the Octopus, Halibut and Killer Whale clans, Raven assembled a small but mighty band of warriors to attack the spirit. Together, they left the coast and headed towards the home of the Southwest Wind.

After two days' journey, they arrived on the island home of the wind spirit. They found the spirit sound asleep in his lodge.

"Our moment has come," whispered Raven. "Halibut, I need to get the spirit to trip and fall. I will make you flat and slippery so that when the spirit steps on you, his back will hit the ground," said Raven, and from then on Halibut was flat, unlike most other fish, which are round.

"Octopus, I want you to get ready to grab the spirit tightly in your many arms after he falls." So Raven used his powers and gave Octopus the ability to grasp and hold onto anything he wanted to.

"Killer Whale, you already possess the strength that will be needed to assist Octopus in dragging the wind spirit to the bottom of the ocean," said Raven. "I will put my plan of action into effect by getting him to run out of the lodge in a hurry."

Raven knew from experience that the Southwest Wind and his brother the North Wind did not like each other, and it was time to exploit that knowledge. "Master of the Southwest Wind," shouted Raven. "I am your brother from the north. Come outside and let us end our rivalry in a battle."

The Southwest Wind spirit was so filled with anger when he rushed out his door that he did not see Halibut on the ground. The wind spirit flew high into the air and landed on his back, then Octopus firmly grasped the spirit and pulled him into the water. Next, Killer Whale grabbed hold of Octopus and pulled them all down to the bottom of the ocean.

Raven then transformed into a fish and swam down to the depths to speak with the spirit.

"Spirit of the Southwest Wind, calm your fury," said Raven. "We have brought you here so that we might come to an agreement."

Struggling in the Octopus' arms, the wind spirit finally calmed down. "I will agree to nothing while I am a prisoner," protested the spirit of the Southwest Wind.

"Ah, but you will," spoke Raven, "for I know that you cannot breathe under water, and if you do not agree to only visit the coast when it is your turn, then I will be forced to keep you down here, where you will die."

With his pride in shambles, the Southwest Wind agreed to calm his fury and only return to the coast during his time. "From this day forth, the Southwest Wind will only bring a warm, gentle breeze to the people and animals of the coast, but if the people forget to offer prayers, then be warned," said the wind spirit.

The promises of the spirit world cannot be broken, and the Southwest Wind returned home to his island to nurse his wounded ego. To this day, the people of the coast remember when Raven fought the Southwest Wind. They speak the name of the spirit softly, for his name carries on the wind, and should they fail to offer him prayers, he will return in anger and blow the people into the air.

The Valley of Shadows

ONCE THERE WAS A WOMAN who had four sons. She was the proudest of mothers and never wanted to see them leave the village, but as with all children, there comes a time when a mother must send them out into the world. To make sure her boys were protected, she threw a magic substance over them to make them strong and brave. She covered three of her sons but missed the youngest one. While the three elder brothers instantly grew strong and courageous, the youngest, who was named Tle'esa, remained weak and child-like.

Every day, Tle'esa watched his brothers leave the village to hunt and return with enough food for everyone. At night, they recounted stories of their adventures in the forest battling great beasts, and everyone in the village listened in reverence to the tales of their courage. It was not easy for Tle'esa. The people of the village always told him that he should be more like his brothers, and the young women laughed at him behind his back when he walked past.

Then, on a day like all the others, the three brothers set off on a hunt into the mountains to catch goats. As these creatures are very timid, the brothers planned to climb up to the highest part of the mountain and wait in the cover of vegetation for the animals to arrive. They planned to set up camp in the evening, and when the sun rose in the morning, they would be waiting for the goats when the animals came to dine on the rich grasses.

The brothers packed enough supplies in their canoes to last for three days and set off for the tribal hunting grounds in the northern mountains. Hiding their canoe in a tiny inlet, the brothers set off in single file up the hillside forests and out onto the slopes of the mountainside. Each carried a bow and arrows, a supply of food and a fur blanket to protect himself against the cold mountain air.

Finally, by late afternoon, they had reached a good height on the mountain. Looking down, they could see the entire valley below encircled by a ridge of snow-capped peaks. After choosing their campsite, the brothers prepared their beds and settled in for the night.

Darkness came upon the brothers slowly as the sun, reluctant to rest, painted the sky a brilliant red. Day gradually gave way to night, and soon, all the three brothers had for company was the starry night sky. The air was cold, but wrapped tightly in their furs, the three men slept soundly.

During the night, the weather began to change, and a thick fog rolled in from the other side of the mountain. The brothers awoke shivering at dawn and could barely see each other in the dense air. They could see neither the valley below nor the mountain peak above. The cold, wet air crept into their hearts as they huddled together and waited for the weather to clear.

But the sun never made it through the mists, and for two days, the brothers remained trapped on the mountainside. They had eaten the last remaining morsels of their supplies, and their furs were now soaked through with water and provided them no comfort from the cold. Together, the brothers prayed for help from the spirits, but as another day came to an end, they remained trapped in the clutches of the thick fog. Lying up against a rock, they huddled together as night closed in around them once more. Strangely enough, sleep came easily for all of them that night.

A strange stillness filled the air when the brothers awoke in the morning. The fog was just beginning to lift, and they could see down into the shadow-covered valley, but no sounds came to their ears. They could hear no wind, though they could see the trees moving, and although they could see birds in the sky, they could not hear their songs. Simply thankful to be out of their predicament, the brothers gave up the hunt and began making their way back down into the valley without looking back to the rock where they had last laid their heads. All the way down the mountainside, the brothers talked of their ordeal and how much they wanted to return home. They were so busy talking that they failed to notice that once they crossed into the shadowy valley, the sun never made it into the sky. It was as though the mountains were blocking out the light.

For several hours, the brothers walked in the direction where they had left the canoe, but as the day came to an end and the shadows fully encircled the valley, the men began looking for a place to spend the night.

Luckily, they came upon a row of lodges on the edge of a stream in the middle of the valley. There were massive, expertly carved totem poles in front of the lodges. But as the brothers approached, no one came out to greet them. Only when the men stopped walking did they realize that they were surrounded by the same eerie stillness they had noticed up on the mountain. They were like men deafened by a loud noise. The brothers could hear neither bird nor wind through the trees, just the sound of their own breathing.

The three men called out, but no one answered. The eldest brother entered one of the lodges, and the mystery of the village was solved at once when he realized that all the homes were deserted. Everywhere, there were signs that Mother Nature was reclaiming the dead village. They saw caved-in roofs and fallen totem poles, but there were none of the familiar scents and sounds of village life. Louder and louder they shouted for someone, anyone, to hear their pleas, but no one came. For many days, the three brothers wandered the village in such a manner, never feeling the desire for food the entire time.

When the eldest brother awoke one morning, the sun once again seemed unable to make it over the mountain ridge, illuminating the sky, with only a faint light reaching the bottom of the valley. As he walked along the paths of the abandoned village, he noticed the shape of a woman in the morning fog.

"Brothers, wake up! There is a spirit woman," said the eldest. "See how she glides just above the ground?"

"Hello, lady, where are you travelling to?" said the second oldest brother.

"I am going to the land of the spirits, sent on this journey by the hand of my husband," she moaned. The brothers could see the tears marking her face as she floated past and into the mists of the forests.

A wave of sadness suddenly swept over the three men. For the next two days, they wept and cried out to the spirits.

〰〰〰

It had been over a year since the three brothers had left the village to hunt goats in mountains, and they still had not returned. The mother of the men lamented the fate of her three strongest boys and hung on to her youngest son tightly.

During that year, however, the once weak son had grown into a strong young man. But Tle'esa's life was not the same without his brothers, and he resolved to discover the reason for their disappearance.

One day, Tle'esa made a fire and called out to the Raven spirit, asking for his help in finding his brothers. As Tle'esa chanted a mournful song of remembrance, Raven suddenly appeared before him. Tle'esa pleaded with Raven to help him learn the fate of his brothers, and Raven agreed to fly up into the sky and search over the lands.

Returning several days later, Raven told Tle'esa that he had looked over the entire world and could find no sign of the missing men.

Despite Raven's news, the young man decided to leave the village and search for his brothers himself. Fearing interference from spirits, Tle'esa was accompanied on his journey by the village shaman, and with his mother's blessing, they set off.

For days, they travelled north until they came upon the canoe his brothers had left hidden in the tiny inlet.

Moments after stepping out of their canoe and onto the valley floor, Tle'esa and the shaman noticed a change in the air. The sunlight had all but disappeared, and there was a strange stillness in the air around them. Walking through the dense forest, they suddenly came upon a clearing and the ruins of an old village. Immediately, Tle'esa was struck by the smell of mustiness and decay that came at him from all directions.

From one of the lodges, Tle'esa heard the sounds of someone moving about. Passing through a beautifully carved entryway, Tle'esa and the shaman saw an old man sitting in the corner by a small fire.

"Come and sit, weary travellers. I am the spirit of this valley of shadows," said the figure through the smoke and faint light of the fire. "You are the brother Tle'esa."

"How did you know that?"

"Your brothers are trapped between worlds. They have become living spirits, occupying neither the land of the living nor the land of the dead," said the old spirit of the valley. "They have walked through this valley in the shadow of death for a year now, crying out their misfortune, but they are unaware that they are no longer whole, for their bodies remain on the mountain, and without a proper burial, they will wander the valley forever, never finding peace."

Upon hearing the old man's words, Tle'esa felt a great sadness at the fate of his brothers, but he resolved to find their final resting place and bring them the peace they deserved. Tle'esa and the shaman climbed up into the mists of the mountain, and after two days of searching, they came upon the rock where his brothers had last rested their heads. After mourning the loss of his brothers, Tle'esa and the shaman ensured that the proper rituals were performed during their burial. After the shaman's final prayer, the three brothers suddenly appeared before Tle'esa and the shaman.

"Little brother, thank you for freeing us from the valley of shadows. We have not had peace for some time now. You who were once weak now are strong, and we owe you our gratitude," spoke the eldest brother.

"You brothers have spent too much time in the valley of shadows and now are spirits of this world," said the shaman. "I will help free you and give you purpose once again."

Staring into the sky with his hands outstretched, the shaman began chanting. Picking up a handful of dirt, he tossed it into the air. Tle'esa watched as his brothers slowly ascended into the heavens to become the three stars that are now known as Orion's belt. Every winter after that, Tle'esa would look up into the sky and know that his brothers were watching out for him and their people.

Thunder and Lightning

IN THE DAYS WHEN the earth was calm and there were no storms, the mighty Thunderbird sat in his cave atop the highest mountain overlooking the sea. He had just woken up from a long slumber and felt a deep hunger in his belly. Peering out into the great waters along the coast, the hungry Thunderbird scanned for his favourite meal of whale. For hours, he gazed out across the dark waters looking for any sign of life.

Nearly ready to give up the search, his eyes grew large when he spotted a huge, grey whale suddenly leap out of the water and into the air. Thunderbird licked his beak and decided that the whale would be his dinner that day. Stretching out his massive wings that could block the sun, Thunderbird pushed off from his perch and soared into the sky.

He flew high up over the whale so as not to alert the creature to his presence. When the whale came up for a breath of air, Thunderbird folded his wings and dove straight for the hapless creature. Without his gaze ever leaving his prey, Thunderbird extended his sharp claws and readied himself to grab the whale out of the water.

However, the whale had seen Thunderbird begin his dive and, not wanting to be anyone's supper, he swam straight to the bottom of the ocean where he could not be reached. Seeing that he had lost his prey at the last second, Thunderbird barely managed to pull out of his dive and swooped back into the air.

In the meantime, the whale had resurfaced and was swimming with all his might out into deeper waters. Thunderbird was not about to give up on his favourite meal and flapped his powerful wings even harder to keep up with the whale. With each stroke of his wings, the air stirred violently all along the coast and into the mountains.

Seeing the great Thunderbird still following, the whale swam faster and faster, trying to escape certain death.

To keep pace with his prey, Thunderbird had to flap his wings harder than he had ever done before. The great wind he created brought the clouds down from the mountains, and soon the sky was completely dark. Along with the gathering clouds and blustering air came a great noise, and each flap of Thunderbird's wings sounded like a great redwood falling in the forest. The sound travelled up and down the coast, sending all the animals running for cover. The noise was so powerful that it shook the water from the clouds and a torrential downpour began falling to the earth. The skies became so dark and stormy that Thunderbird could no longer see his prey. He was so angry at losing the whale that powerful bolts of light began shooting from his eyes.

Each time the bolts shot out of his eyes, Thunderbird could just make out the shadow of the whale beneath the waves.

For several hours, Thunderbird pursued the whale through the darkness, rain and wind. The conditions had become so bad that the whale completely lost sight of Thunderbird. Surfacing to try to catch a glimpse of his pursuer, the whale failed to notice Thunderbird diving from the cover of the clouds with his talons extended. In one quick swoop, Thunderbird caught the whale and began making his way back to his lair.

When Thunderbird finally landed in his lair and closed his mighty wings, everything became still again. The wind died down, the clouds returned to their home in the mountains, and the sun reappeared, shining its light down on earth again.

As Thunderbird devoured his well-earned meal, he realized that he might not have had to work so hard had the whale not seen him attack in the first place. From that time on, he decided that he would use his powerful wings to stir up strong winds and bring in the heavy clouds from the mountains to darken the skies. Only then would he use the bolts of lightning from his eyes to show him the way to his prey.

So now, every time the skies darken and a storm develops, you know that Thunderbird is hungry and out searching for his next meal.

Mink Tries to Take a Wife

—————≈≈≈≈≈≈—————

IN THE TIME WHEN THE SPIRITS ruled the earth, there came a day when Ka'iq, Mink, decided to take a wife. So Ka'iq approached an Eagle maiden and said, "Will you come and be my wife and live with me?"

"You can't become my husband. How will you fly to the ocean to catch salmon, when you have no wings?" the Eagle maiden responded.

"Well," said Ka'iq. "You will lend me your magic coat of Eagle feathers, and I will fly by your side."

The Eagle maiden agreed that Ka'iq's plan would work, and the two became husband and wife.

One day, the couple was sitting high up in a tree looking out over the water. Patiently, Eagle stared out across the waters, waiting for the seasonal arrival of the salmon. With her great vision, Eagle peered out into the ocean and saw the salmon approaching the coast.

"It is time, husband," said Eagle. She gave Mink a coat of feathers so that he could fly and join her on the hunt. But before taking to the air, Ka'iq's wife warned him, "Now husband, be careful. When you see your prey from above, do not dive down too fast, but fly steady and strong or else you will miss your target." At that, Mink promised to follow his wife's instructions, and they pushed off from their perch and flew out over the water.

After circling high above the ocean for a few moments, Mink spotted his first salmon, and forgetting the warnings of his wife, he dove at maximum speed towards the fish. Alerted to his presence by the sudden movement, the salmon were able to get away before Mink hit the water at full speed. He hit the water so hard that he lost his coat of feathers. Eagle was disappointed at her husband's clumsy attempt to fish, so she collected her coat of feathers and flew back to her nest alone. Mink was again without a wife.

Still nursing his bruised ego after losing Eagle, Ka'iq wandered the mountain forest to the north looking for a new wife. After some time, he came upon Mountain Lion.

"Will you consent to be my wife?" asked Ka'iq.

"You are too small," replied Mountain Lion. "I need a husband who can aid in the hunt and help feed my children."

"That is no problem," said the boastful Ka'iq, "for I make up for my size with great cunning. No prey has yet escaped my clutches."

"Well then, if that is the case, I accept your offer to become my husband," replied Mountain Lion.

For the remaining days of summer, Ka'iq and his wife, Mountain Lion, lived in happiness and welcomed a new baby into their family. But as summer gave way to fall and then winter, hunting for prey was becoming difficult for Ka'iq as all the smaller animals went into hiding at the appearance of the first snow, leaving only the larger animals such as moose and elk. After not having a meal for more than a month, Ka'iq's Mountain Lion wife began to complain about her husband's inability to provide for the family. Soon her children were so hungry that she had to brave the cold and snow to bring back food. With her great size and powerful claws, Mountain Lion had no problem attacking the larger prey.

One day, after returning to her lair with a fresh kill of elk, she spoke to her useless husband. "Every day I go out and find food for the family while you stay at home. You eat my food and bring nothing home," she said angrily.

Ka'iq tried to calm his wife by caressing her, but she beat him and threw him into the snow.

Wandering along the coast lamenting his lack of a wife, Ka'iq came upon a lovely beach and met a beautiful Sea-Wolf swimming in the shallow waters. She was the Sea-Wolf princess and one of the most beautiful creatures in all the known lands.

"Sea-Wolf princess," said Ka'iq loudly over the crashing waves. "I am in search of a wife, and you are the most beautiful in all the lands. Will you be my wife?"

"You are but one of many suitors who have asked for my affections," said Sea-Wolf proudly, pointing to the courtyard where Bear Chief and Eagle Chief stood. "I possess a beauty that is desired by men, and therefore, to win my heart, you must prove your worth to me."

Ka'iq did not have the strength of the Bear clan nor the swiftness of the Eagle clan, but he did have cunning, and it would be with this, his greatest gift, that he would win her heart.

Although Ka'iq had much confidence in his abilities, the suitors from the Bear and Eagle clans thought themselves to be the only true contenders for Sea-Wolf's heart.

The suitor from the Bear clan possessed mighty strength and he shook the earth, breaking apart the mainland into many islands.

"I have created many islands for you, where countless seals will come to raise their young and you will hunt them until you are full," said Bear with zealous confidence.

"Impressive, but you are too rough for me. Your claws might one day accidentally tear me to pieces. I need a husband with a steady hand," said Sea-Wolf.

The suitor from the Eagle clan stood and said, "My princess of the Sea-Wolves, you must choose me, for I fly strong and steady, but I am best known for my swiftness. For proof of my worthiness, I shall collect for you as many seals as I can carry."

Leaving his perch high in the trees, Eagle soared into the sky. With one swift beat of his wings, he moved across the coastline at a speed too fast to see. Picking them out of the sea and off the rocks, Eagle collected over a hundred seals in his great talons and powerful beak.

"It is has taken me three beats of your heart to return with more seals than you could catch in a month. I, princess, and I alone am worthy of your heart," said Eagle confidently.

"While you may have caught me my dinner, I do not require someone to hunt for me. I am the Wolf of the Sea, the most feared predator in the ocean. The hunt gives strength to my spirit," said Sea-Wolf. "I cannot marry you, member of the Eagle clan."

Ka'iq, observing the two suitors fail, knew the Sea-Wolf clan admired cunning and intelligence. "Princess, where these two suitors have failed, I will triumph. I do not possess Bear's strength or Eagle's speed, but I possess cunning like no other. For my proof of worthiness, I shall catch a salmon without moving."

Ka'iq waded into the waters and called out to the salmon, "Please come to me. I just want to play." Two salmon appeared, but nervous creatures by nature, they stayed some distance away from the shore. "No, that isn't close enough, come closer so that we will able to have fun," said Ka'iq. The salmon moved in a little closer, but only after he had called four more times were the salmon close enough for Ka'iq to kill them. Now he had two salmon, one for the princess and one for himself, and he greedily ate his up. But with a full belly, Ka'iq could not resist falling asleep before giving his potential bride her prize. While he was sleeping, Raven appeared and stole the other salmon from him. But before he ran off, Raven rubbed Ka'iq's teeth with the fish, leaving little bits behind. When Ka'iq awoke, he saw that his salmon was gone, but before he cried out, he tasted salmon on his tongue and he had salmon roe between his teeth.

"Oh no! I must have eaten my bride's salmon!" exclaimed Ka'iq. "I must catch her another." It took two more days to catch another salmon, and when he returned to the home of the Sea-Wolf princess, another was there to greet him.

"It matters not what you have done, Ka'iq," said Raven. "For I was the one who stole your salmon. While you were sleeping, I rubbed the fish on your teeth so that you would think you ate the salmon. I used your ignorance to my advantage, and therefore I, Raven, am the most cunning of them all. The Sea-Wolf princess has chosen to marry me."

With downcast eyes, Ka'iq walked away from the coast.

Ka'iq wandered into a lush green valley to the east, whereupon he came to a lake. At the water's edge, he caught a glimpse of the most beautiful woman he had ever seen, bathing in the shallow waters. Ka'iq desired this woman, but he knew that she would never marry him. So he transformed into a trout and swam up under the woman's legs and made her pregnant. Her belly swelled to a great size, and the following morning, she gave birth to a son. Everyone questioned the beautiful woman as to the identity of the father, but not even she knew who had made her child.

The women of the village thought that the father might be Crane, so they brought the child to his lodge and made him hold the baby. "If the child is yours, he will give you a great gift," said the beautiful woman. As Crane held the child, it started to dirty him, but when the mother went to clean the child, she found that her boy had left behind a pile of bronze. "You cannot be the father, for bronze is not a gift of the spirits," said the beautiful woman.

Next she went to the home of Raven. "The child must be yours, great Raven. You are to known to father many children. Please take the baby, and he will reveal if you are his father," said the beautiful woman, handing Raven her child. The child at once began to dirty Raven, leaving behind a pile of shiny gold.

Ka'iq, knowing that he was the father of the child, was curious to see what riches the child would leave for his true father and snatched the baby from Raven. "I am your father, child. Give me riches," said Ka'iq. The child began to dirty Ka'iq, but he left behind neither gold nor bronze. Raven then cried out "Caw! Caw! Caw! Ka'iq, you most certainly are not the father!" and everyone began to laugh at him.

Ka'iq searched throughout the warm nights of summer and into the cooler days of fall, but still had found no wife. Tired after months of searching, Ka'iq found a comfortable nest and fell into a deep slumber for the winter, but not before declaring that he would try to find a wife again come spring.

The Origin of The Loon

ONCE THERE WERE TWO BROTHERS who grew up as rivals. Throughout their formative years, they would make a competition out of anything, just to see who would win. They would race down to the beach, compete to build the best canoe or see who could catch the biggest halibut. Their competitiveness knew no bounds, but as the fresh-faced youths became young men, their attentions turned naturally to the affections of women.

Near the young men's village, there happened to be a lake, and for generations, the shamans had forbidden the people to even go near the water because it was believed that within its dark, murky waters lay the home of an evil spirit. The brothers knew the stories—tales of villagers taking a swim on a hot day and never returning or women going to fetch water and simply disappearing. It was believed that the spirit at the bottom of the lake had fallen in many years ago and, angry that no one had tried to rescue him, he began pulling people under.

The stories of the evil spirit in the lake had scared the two brothers when they were young, but now that they were grown up, they no longer believed in "silly children's tales," as they often called them.

One evening, as the two brothers were walking near the forbidden lake, a strange fog suddenly rolled in along the forest floor. The sun had set behind a mountain, and the brothers could only see through the trees by the faint light of the moon. Both men felt a sudden rush of panic, but neither wanted to admit to the other that he was frightened. All those childhood stories of evil spirits came rushing back to them.

It was at that moment that the elder brother saw something in the distance through the fog and the dense forest. He wasn't sure at first what it was and neither was the younger brother, but as they cautiously approached, they could make out the silhouette of a woman. Her sweet fragrance drifted on the wind directly to the senses of the brothers. Curiosity and something unknown flooded through their bodies.

The two enchanted brothers came to a small clearing in the woods and saw a beautiful woman sitting on a large rock. She had the longest, darkest hair they had ever seen and the smoothest skin. She beckoned to them to approach. Held captive by her beauty, the brothers did as they were instructed.

"Who are you and where did you come from?" asked the elder brother.

"It matters not who I am or where I came from," replied the beautiful siren in a whisper. "What matters is that you find me desirable."

The brothers responded with a simple nod of their heads. Although they wanted to know where the woman came from, there was a stronger force urging them forward.

"Unfortunately, I cannot decide which one of you I will choose," said the woman, pointing between the two brothers with her slender finger. "What we need is a test of strength and courage to prove to me which one of you wants me the most.

"I will do anything to win your love," said the elder brother.

"I will do whatever is necessary," replied the younger.

"Excellent. Then whichever one of you makes it across the lake first will win me as his prize," she said with a slight smile.

The two brothers walked straight out of the forest without saying a word to each other all the way down to the lake. The stories of people disappearing did not even enter their minds. The only thing each man desired was to win the contest and claim his treasure.

At the other end of the lake, the brothers saw the glowing figure of the woman. She appeared to be floating above the surface of the water. They both desired her as they had never desired anything before. Without further hesitation, the elder brother jumped into the cold lake, followed quickly by his sibling.

After the first few strokes, the older brother had a good lead and was clearly the better swimmer. With only a short distance to victory, he felt an invisible hand pull at his feet. Looking down, he could see an evil spirit holding onto him and pulling him under the water.

"Ah, foolish boy," said the evil spirit. "I have you in my grasp now. I have been lonely for so many years. I think I will make you a prisoner of this lake so that you might keep me company."

The elder brother pleaded with the spirit for his freedom, and it seemed that his words found an understanding ear.

"I hear your pain, young one. But I shall not remain alone," said the evil spirit. "You have a choice: either you stay with me and allow your brother to win the race and the heart of the beautiful maiden, or you must give me your brother as my prize and I shall set you free so that you may have your heart's desire."

The elder brother thought for a moment and replied, "I have considered your offer, and I will give you my brother as your prize."

The evil spirit released the elder brother at once. He swam to the surface and looked about to see if he could spot his sibling, but there was no one.

The younger brother was now under the water, face to face with the evil spirit. "Young one, your brother has given you to me. Because of his pride and lust for a woman, he has sold his own blood into slavery. You will be my prisoner for all eternity," laughed the evil spirit. "I will now transform you into a loon, and you will be my entertainment."

With a wave of the spirit's hand, the young man had wings instead of arms, a beak instead of a mouth and feathers where there once had been skin.

"But I am not without feeling. I will give you a voice that will be both beautiful and haunting. You may use your song to tell others of your great despair."

The younger brother swam up to the surface in his new form and immediately began his plaintive cry. It echoed around the lake and onto the ears of his brother.

Finally reaching the other end of the lake, the older brother walked onto the shore with pride in his eyes and a desire in his heart to claim his prize. But instead of a beautiful woman, he found the evil spirit that had pulled him underwater.

"You are an extremely foolish boy. Don't you see that you have been deceived? It was I who transformed myself into the woman and lured you down to my lake, and now you have given your brother to me for eternity. He knows now of your betrayal and will sing his sorrowful song for the rest of time."

Finally released from the spell of the evil spirit, the older brother awoke to the reality of what he had done. He looked out across the water of the lake and saw his brother, the loon, swimming along, slowly calling out his despair to the world. Unable to return to the village because of the shame he would bring to his family, the older brother walked into the forest and was never heard from again.

To this day, the loon still sings of the time that a brother blinded by lust and pride was deceived into trading his freedom for that of his sibling.

The Woman of the Nass River Volcano

IT CAME TO PASS ONE DAY that the nephew of the Bear clan chief aspired to marry the daughter of the Salmon clan chief. Mortal enemies long before the memories of the oldest tribesman, the two chiefs decided that the marriage would serve to unite the warring tribes and bring peace to the land once and for all. No sooner had the chiefs agreed to the union than messengers were sent with an official proposal of marriage from the nephew.

Accepting the responsibility of bringing peace to her people, the daughter of the Salmon clan chief prepared herself to be taken to her new home. Because she was of high standing in the village, the emissaries of the Bear clan arrived at the Salmon clan village in two wonderfully carved and decorated canoes. When the daughter exited her lodge, every villager stopped to admire her beauty and splendour. The chief embraced his daughter one last time, and she left to go to her new life with the Bear clan, where she would be treated as one of the highest ranking members of the clan and would soon become the bride of a future chief.

Arriving at the Bear clan village, she was greeted by the chief and her young suitor. Days passed in ceremony and feasting until everything eventually settled down and the normal rhythm of life took over. But all was not happy in the newlyweds' home. The nephew had begun beating his wife and dishonouring her character by bedding other women. The Salmon chief's daughter could do nothing about her unhappy situation and, out of shame, she soon secluded herself away from the village in the mountains. She stayed in her tent for months, wailing and mourning her ill-fated marriage. Her husband visited her on occasion, and within a few months, her belly began to swell. But still she remained in her tent away from the village.

The news of her unhappiness reached the ears of her father, the Salmon clan chief. He quickly assembled a war party and made for the village of the Bear clan to avenge the dishonour done to his daughter and his people. The Bear clan and the Salmon clan shed much blood in their warring.

In the fury of war, the Salmon clan bathed the Bear clan's lands in a hellish fire, and its rage consumed the entire Bear village.

Led by the chief, the surviving members of the Salmon clan scattered into the forests above the village to search for the chief's daughter. They hoped she had escaped the bloodshed and fire, but when they came upon her tent, they found it completely burned. The only thing that escaped the flames was a wooden statue of a salmon that had somehow survived the fire. The chief's daughter and her unborn child were nowhere to be found.

Because she had died alone and in such despair, her spirit remained on earth, and she became the spirit of the mountain upon which she had taken her last breath.

Ashamed at having lost his daughter and his unborn grandchild, the Salmon clan chief lamented his tribe's actions. "I fear a new danger is now in store for us as punishment for our rash behaviour. My daughter is angry, and her spirit will seek retribution on us all for abandoning her. She might sleep long, but one day, she will wake and remember what we have done to her and her child," said the Salmon clan chief.

From that day onwards, the people of the Bear clan and the Salmon clan said many prayers and offered up sacrifices to the woman's spirit, but as time passed, the memory of the chief's daughter faded. The people sometimes felt a tremor at the foot of the mountain or heard a mournful song on the tail of the wind, but her story had been forgotten.

~~~~~~~

In the early springtime, five young men from the Bear clan paddled upstream in a canoe to their favourite fishing spot. Once they reached the place, the men settled under the shade of a tree and began to fish.

Each time one of their spears pierced the flesh of a salmon, the men heard the cries of a woman from high up the mountain. The wisest of the five fishermen said, "This is an ill omen for us. Let us depart from this land."

But no one heeded the warnings, and the men continued to fish.

They speared another salmon, and the voice called down from the mountain, even louder this time, "My child, my child, give me back my child! What have you done with my child? You shall pay for your arrogance," echoed the voice of a woman.

Upon hearing the ghostly words of the unknown woman, the five men packed up their fishing gear and headed back to their village with the utmost speed. But once they had returned to the relative safety of the village, the five men forgot what had happened on the mountain. But the spirit had been awoken and did not like the men of the Bear clan fishing on her lands. Her mournful song drifted down from the mountain, along the river and wafted through the village like a storm. All the villagers could hear her wailing, but none of them paid her any attention, except one old man.

"Perhaps one of our young people has broken a taboo and upset a spirit," suggested the old Bear clan tribesman. "We should leave the area now before something evil befalls our people." But the words of the old man fell on deaf ears, proving that even with eyes, one might still be blind. Something inside the old man told him to make preparations and leave the village. Somewhere in his mind he could remember his grandfather telling him the story of the woman of the fire mountain, and that was enough to send him to seek cover.

The very next night after the old man's departure, the people of the Bear clan village heard a distant rumbling. Again the wind wailed, "Where's my child? Where's my child!" But no one heeded the call. The rumblings grew louder and louder, until finally, smoke began to spew forth from the top of the mountain, and a blazing river of fire poured down from the peak. It was only then that the people realized the danger and tried to escape, but the river of molten rock had already consumed the canoes. With all avenues of escape blocked, the entire Bear clan perished in the flames.

Only the old man who had escaped into the forest survived. He remained in his hiding place for many days, waiting for the fury of the mountain to calm down. Once the smoke and dust had cleared, the old man emerged from the cave in which he had been hiding. The land that stretched out before him lay covered in smouldering black rock. Nearly all the trees had been burned, and no sound of life could be heard. He called out for someone to come to his aid, but the only voice he heard was that of the crying woman. "I have avenged my death and the death of my child now. As I was destroyed by fire, so have your people been destroyed," the voice moaned. "Go forth and tell all of my fury, and if anyone should upset me in my lands again, I will bring forth a vengeance on the world that will consume everything in fire."

For days, the old man wandered through the scorched landscape. Over blazing hot rocks and with no cover from the sun, he marched on. Finally, on the verge of starvation, he walked into the ancestral home of the Salmon clan. Unlike their Bear brethren, the Salmon clan had escaped the fiery fury of the volcano spirit. Exhausted, the old man collapsed at the entrance to the village.

After two days' rest, the old man had regained enough energy to speak. "How did your village survive the fury of the mountain?" he asked.

"Distinguished member of the Bear clan," said the Salmon clan chief. "Long ago, our descendants erred by sending the most beautiful woman in our village to live with the Bear clan to unite our people and bring peace. But she was mistreated and neglected by her new family. In our blind search for revenge on the Bear clan, a war broke out, and as a result, the woman died a fiery, painful death on the side of that very mountain. Since then, our people have told her story, and every day we offer prayers to her spirit and ask her for forgiveness. The foolish Bear clan forgot their history, and now all your people are gone."

The old man began to weep on hearing the words of the chief.

"You are the last of your tribe, so perhaps now the daughter of the Salmon clan will be at peace. But we will continue to honour her memory and pray for her lest her angry spirit return for further vengeance."

That night, a ceremony was held and a totem pole was raised to commemorate the fury of the Volcano Woman and the destruction of the Bear clan.

Killer Whale and the Wife

GUNARH WAS A GREAT and revered hunter. Because of his prowess on the hunt, he had earned the respect of his entire village and the love of its most beautiful woman.

One day, while Gunarh was out fishing for halibut with several other men from the village, he noticed a huge black fin suddenly break the surface of the water.

Upon seeing the great fin, the men ceased paddling. The great beast began to circle the boat cautiously, creating ripples in the water that rocked the boat from side to side. All the men knew very well to whom the black fin belonged. It was that of the great sea-wolf, Killer Whale.

Killer Whale did not seem to intend any harm to Gunarh and his fishermen, but the creature was acting in an unusual manner by repeatedly circling the canoe. Gunarh could see that Killer Whale's actions were making some of the men nervous.

When Killer Whale came a little closer to the boat, one of the fishermen picked up a stone that they were using for ballast and threw it at the giant creature. It struck the fin of the beast, but Killer Whale did not even flinch upon the stone's impact. Sensing some innocent sport at hand, Gunarh and the rest of the crew started throwing the other ballast stones.

One strike with a stone was tolerable, but when hit with a volley of rocks, Killer Whale went wild. Clearly angry with the fishermen, Killer Whale stopped circling the men and headed directly for the shores of the village. Gunarh quickly gave orders to the men to start paddling and head straight for the beast. But their paddles could not keep pace with the furious Killer Whale, who reached the beach in just three strokes of his massive tail. Gunarh and the fisherman were still far away from the beach, but he could clearly see his beautiful wife on the shore busy washing furs. He tried to warn her of the approaching beast, but the crashing of the waves washed away his cries.

Killer Whale emerged from the waters with a splash and carried Gunarh's wife away on his back. Gunarh could do nothing but watch his wife's horrified face as she clung to the dorsal fin of the monster. She managed to cry out, "My husband! Come rescue me!" before she disappeared beneath the waves and was not seen again.

Gunarh immediately rushed to the village and took his hunting weapons, intent on rescuing his wife from the clutches of the beast. Putting his things in his canoe, he pushed off from shore and headed to the spot where he had last seen his wife. Preparing to enter the watery domain of Killer Whale, Gunarh tied a long line to the canoe and, holding on to it, dived down to the bottom of the sea.

When he reached the bottom, he came upon the Cormorant people. Killer Whale had taken them from the surface and made them his prisoners. Without hesitation, Gunarh cut the bonds that tied the Cormorants and set them free.

"Thank you, great hunter," said one of the Cormorants. "For your kindness towards us, we can tell you that your wife has been taken to the lodge of Killer Whale over yonder. Take this piece of wood and throw it into the fire. It will give you time to escape. Go now, for we Cormorants must plan our revenge."

Thanking the Cormorant people, Gunarh took the magical piece of wood and made his way to the home of Killer Whale. Following the path the Cormorants had shown him, he came upon a grand lodge in the middle of a clearing. Approaching the lodge, he sought cover behind a pile of rocks. As he watched the lodge, he saw his wife through one of the windows. Anger began to boil inside him when he saw that she was dressed in the rags of a slave. He prayed that the wood he had been given had some incredible magical powers because he could see that Killer Whale and his many concubines surrounded his wife.

Not able to wait one moment longer, Gunarh crashed through the door and threw the magical piece of wood onto the fire. As soon as the wood touched the flame, white smoke began to fill the room. In the confusion, Gunarh grabbed his wife and pulled her out of the lodge. But before exiting the door, Gunarh took some magical snuff from his pocket and placed it in the mouth of one of the Killer Whale's concubines. The magical snuff made the concubine swell to an enormous size, blocking the door and stopping Killer Whale from pursuing Gunarh and his wife. The other concubines urinated on her to shrink her, but by the time she was small enough for Killer Whale to get past, Gunarh and his wife had escaped. Killer Whale and his concubines ran after the couple, but just as they were about to overtake Gunarh and his wife, the Cormorants sprang their trap.

They released a poison in the water between the whales and Gunarh that confused the pursuers so that they could not remember why they were chasing the humans. The distraction allowed Gunarh and his wife to reach his canoe and return to their village.

Back in the safety of their village, Gunarh turned to his wife. "I'm sorry," he said. "It was because of our silly game of throwing rocks at the fin of the great beast that you were taken. Now I know never to anger something bigger than myself."

The Princess and the Bears

ONE DAY, the people of the Nass River Valley were out catching sockeye during the annual salmon season and were busy cleaning and drying their catch on the banks. This was also the time of year when the bushes were full of delicious salmon berries. One sunny afternoon, the beautiful princess said to her friends, "Let us go into the mountain forest and pick salmon berries."

The next day, the princess and her friends took their berry baskets and went up the mountainside to fetch the sweet fruit. The group went into the bushes, and gradually they wandered farther and farther apart from one another, each going where the berries were ripe and plentiful.

Walking along a sunlit path, the princess soon found herself all alone. But she did not fear any evil creature or harm from another tribe; her mind was simply occupied by the splendour around her. Enthralled by the beauty of nature, she failed to notice a pile of bear excrement on the trail. She stepped in it and smeared it with her foot. This made the princess extremely angry. "That dirty, filthy beast of a bear," she cursed out loud. "The foul creatures should mind where they sit."

All day, as the princess and her friends wandered through the forest, she would not stop talking about the incident and how bears were such disgusting creatures. At the top of her lungs, the princess decried the foulness of all bears. All the while, she wandered farther and farther into the forest in search of the precious salmon berries. While her friends had all filled their baskets to the brim and returned to the canoe, the princess still wandered in the woods, quietly muttering nasty things about the bears.

Finally, she finished filling her basket and began making her way down to the canoe. But her basket was so heavy that the strap broke and the berries spilled out onto the forest floor. She called out for her friends to help, but no one came. Unable to get her berries back to the canoe, she began to weep and bemoan her misfortune. "The bears have cursed me, and now I cannot get my berries back to the village. This is not how a princess should be treated!"

Just when she had reached the point of giving up and returning to the canoe empty-handed, two handsome young men suddenly appeared and offered their assistance. "Princess, we were sent here to aid you. We heard your cries from afar and have come to lead you through the forest so that no harm may befall such a beautiful young woman," said one of the men.

The princess did not know the men nor what tribe they came from, but she could not find any reason to suspect such handsome and helpful young men. She was so enraptured by them that she did not notice they were leading her away from where her friends were waiting with the canoe. Deeper and deeper into the forest they led her, but the princess never noticed because she was too busy laughing and flirting with the handsomer of the two men.

It wasn't long until they came to a clearing in the forest where stood the largest village she had ever seen. The men escorted the princess to a lodge in the centre of the village, and the handsomer of the two men said, "Please do not leave until I have spoken to my father inside. It will only be a minute, beautiful princess."

Still no fear ran through her veins, until she heard the booming voice of the father from inside the lodge.

"Did you find what I asked for?" said the voice.

"Yes, father, she waits outside. You will be most pleased."

"Bring her to me so that I might lay my eyes on my new prisoner."

The young man came out of the lodge and took the princess in to see the man with the booming voice. Inside the lodge, it became obvious to the princess that she was in the presence of the chief of the village. At the end of the room was one of the largest men she had ever laid her eyes upon. Beside him sat several women dressed in bearskin garments, and many slaves scurried about tending to their needs.

"Come, beautiful princess, and sit next to me so that we might talk about why you were brought here," said the chief.

Terror filled the heart of the princess as she finally realized what was to become of her. Trying to escape seemed futile because she had not paid attention to the path they had taken through the forest. A wave of grief overcame her.

"While you were in the forest, you were heard to denounce the Bear people. You will join the others that have dishonoured our people," said the chief.

The chief called his people to assembly, and the entire village came out to see their new guest. The princess was sitting quietly behind him when she felt a pinch on her thigh. Looking down, she saw a little old woman staring back up at her. "I am Mouse Woman," she said in her squeaky voice. "You have been taken against your will. They heard your insults throughout the entire forest, and to make matters worse, the excrement you stepped in was that of the Bear chief. Have you any wool or fat as a gift for me? If you do, then I can help you escape."

Scared at what might happen to her for insulting the chief, the princess agreed to the demands of Mouse Woman and gave her the wool earrings she had been wearing and some mountain goat fat that she used to keep her skin soft. She handed the items to the tiny woman, who grabbed them and scurried off. The princess, thinking she had just been the victim of a trick, began sobbing, but her hopes were restored when Mouse Woman returned.

"Oh, please help me. What do they intend to do with me?" asked the princess.

"The prince of the Bears intends to take you as his wife," said Mouse Woman. "But be warned—this will not be a marriage based on love. Do you see all the old slaves about you? They were taken away by the Bears for making fun of them in the same way you did. I have seen many perish for breaking the laws of the Bear people."

"But they cannot do this. I am the princess of my people," said the young woman, who again started to cry. "Please help me get out of here and back to my people."

"Okay, princess, but you must follow my instructions carefully," whispered Mouse Woman. "When you go into the forest to relieve yourself, you must dig a hole and hide your excrement. As soon as you cover it up, take a piece off your copper bracelet and place it on top of the pile as if it was your excrement. You must do this every time, for if you don't, they will consider you worthless and kill you."

The princess agreed to follow Mouse Woman's instructions even though they were very strange. Over the next few days, there was a great deal of activity in the Bear clan village. Inside their lodges, the people walked about normally, but when they went out into the sun, they would don their Bear garments and walk about as animals. The princess was kept in a small room in the lodge of the chief's son and not allowed to go anywhere by herself.

But soon the princess needed to go outside. She excused herself and went into the bushes where she relieved herself. Then she covered it up and put a piece from one of her copper bracelets on top of the earth. As she returned to the lodge, she noticed that she was being followed. A man from the Bear clan rushed over to where she had relieved herself and was surprised to find a piece of copper.

"The princess has good reason to laugh at our excrement. She has produced copper excrement, so she must be an exceptional person," the man said.

Picking up the piece of copper, the man ran to the chief and showed him what the princess had produced.

"The princess was right to make fun of our excrement," said the chief of the Bear clan. "She must be a person of great stature and descended from the spirits. I have decided that she will wed my son and become my daughter-in-law."

The princess was glad that she was not to become a slave, but she desperately wanted to go home. However, any thoughts of escape had to be put aside because of the Bear people's ability to track their prey.

After much preparation, the princess and the chief's son were wed and began living together as husband and wife. At first, the people of the village did not welcome the princess, but in time, they began to take to the newest member of the clan. Although her life was not unbearable, the princess still longed for her village and to see her father once again.

All was quiet one day, when two members of the Bear clan rushed into the lodge of the chief. "One of our brothers has been shot and killed by a hunter!" said the Bear clan member. "They are the Nass River people. I fear they are still searching for their princess. For the next few months, keep our people on alert for I know them to be a war-like people," said the Bear chief.

Many months had passed since the Bear clan had taken the princess and married her to the chief's son. As the days began to shorten and the chill of winter approached, the princess' belly began to swell with child. Worried that she might never see her family once she gave birth, she asked Mouse Woman to find her family and see if they were still looking for her. When Mouse Woman returned, she brought the news that the princess' tribe had never given up hope of finding her.

"A few months ago, they discovered your tracks leading away from where you were last seen picking berries," said Mouse Woman. "They know that you have been taken, and they have been searching for you all this time. That is why not too long ago, a member of the Bear clan was killed."

The princess' heart filled with joy at the news of her tribe's ongoing search for her, but escape was still not an option, and now that she was pregnant, rescue seemed unlikely.

Soon it was time for the Bears to retire to their caves in the mountains and sleep for the winter. The chief's son had selected a perfect spot well out of the way of the hunters so that his bride might give birth to his cubs in peace. Her only hope now was that her father, the best hunter in her village, could find her and bring her home.

Through the forest, the princess' father searched and searched for any sign of his precious daughter. It had been many months since her disappearance, and there had been neither sight nor sound of her. Thinking something was not right, he continued day after day to comb the forest, searching for any clue, until one day in early winter, he came upon the basket that belonged to the princess. He almost jumped into the air with joy when he realized that his daughter might still be alive. Beside the basket were two sets of footprints in the mud belonging to the two men who had led her away. The chief saw the direction in which the tracks headed and knew at once that they pointed towards the land of the Bear clan. Setting out to find his daughter, the chief followed the tracks to the Bear's village. But it was empty. The Bear people had already left for their winter dens in the mountains. Following the same path through the woods, the princess' father travelled up into the hills for two days through wind, snow and difficult terrain.

From a small clearing below, he could see a series of cave openings up on a high ridge. It seemed the most likely place for bears to winter. That was when he saw his daughter appear from the mouth of a cave with two babies in her arms.

Rushing over to her, he embraced her tightly. "I thought you were dead," he said. "Let us leave this place now before we are seen."

"Father, I cannot leave so suddenly for I have given life to two children. And although I have been held here against my will, I have come love my husband. Please treat his death with respect," said the princess.

The father then built a fire in front of the cave mouth in order to smoke out his daughter's Bear husband. Soon the prince of the Bears was overcome by the smell of fire.

"I see now that my fate is sealed. You have been wronged, great chief, and I will suffer for my tribe's blindness," said the prince of the Bear clan. "As my final offering of peace, I give you two great sons who will make you wealthy for they shall become great hunters. But when you are old and eventually pass into the next world, you must promise to allow them to return to their people."

The princess' father agreed and then killed Bear with a spear to the heart. As soon as her husband hit the ground, the princess fell to her knees and sang of his greatness.

Returning to the village, the princess related the story of her capture to her father. Her father had a totem pole erected in front of the village in honour of the princess' heroism.

As for the twin children, they spent many years with their mother in her village. During the days when the light lasts the longest, their mother allowed them to don their Bear garments and run about the woods and meadows in their native dress, but in their lodge, the garments were removed and two regular boys would roam the house. As the children grew, they became the best hunters in the village and made the chief very wealthy. But the day eventually came when the chief, the Bear twins' grandfather, died in his sleep. It was time for the princess to honour the promise she had made to her husband, and she watched as her children left her side and returned to the lands of the Bear clan, where they stayed forever.

Thunderbird Fights Raven

DURING THE DAYS when the land was filled with danger and terror, a mighty spirit, Thunderbird, lived very high up in the mountains and clouds, looming above the valleys and the coast, always waiting to unleash his anger and fury on the creatures below.

Every living thing was filled with fear when Thunderbird's booming roar sounded across the skies and his lightning gaze peered into every shadow underneath the darkness of the clouds. With a wink of his eye, a flash of lightning fire spewed forth and illuminated the earth below. No living thing escaped his gaze. He was the most powerful being in all the known lands, and as it goes when a single being has all the power, Thunderbird became a tyrant to the people.

Seated upon the highest peak of the darkest mountain, when he saw someone venture out into the open, he immediately spread dark clouds above him and thundered so loudly as to make the earth shake. He had terrible rages and would often randomly strike someone out of existence. A state of constant fear of Thunderbird and the unknown kept the people in their homes. Under the reign of Thunderbird, all life had to bow before his might.

It came to be one day that Raven found himself far away from his home and in the lands of a people in dire straits.

"What has put you noble people in such a state?" asked Raven. "What has reduced such a brave tribe to its knees?"

The people related in detail how they were under the tyranny of Thunderbird and that it had been many days since they were last able to fish the waters or hunt in the forests. Looking up at the highest peak, Raven could see the place that Thunderbird called home. A dark bank of clouds encircled Thunderbird's mountain perch. Flashes of light above the clouds signalled that the great Thunderbird spirit was awake and watching.

Raven could not turn his back on the people and allow the tyrant to control the world. He declared to the people that he would come to their aid and bring Thunderbird's tyranny to an end.

For the next three days, Raven stayed deep in the forest to meditate on his plan for approaching Thunderbird. By the time he left the woods, Raven had come up with a brilliant scheme.

Transforming himself into a light, downy feather, Raven floated up on the wind towards the home of Thunderbird. Pushed up high in the sky by a warm current of air, the feather twisted and turned in the wind, catching Thunderbird's all-seeing eye.

"What a strange feather," said Thunderbird. "It looks like the plumage of a bird, and yet it looks kind of like a man."

Thunderbird then rose into the air to get a better look at the strange object floating above his lair. "I will produce some rain and see what this little feather can do against my powers."

Thunderbird let out a tremendous bellow that shook the rain from the clouds, down onto the little feather. But the magic feather did not fall from the sky. When the rain stopped, the feather magically rose up before the eyes of Thunderbird and began to shoot out thunder and lightning at an incredible rate. Thunderbird looked on in amazement that such a small, delicate feather could produce so much fury.

"I thought I was the only one in the known world able to produce such violent storms," said Thunderbird with a hint of jealousy.

Then Thunderbird rained down a volley of thunder and lightning on the little feather, expecting it to bow to his might, but the little feather answered back with a greater display of fire and sound. Determined not to be outclassed by such a puny antagonist, Thunderbird flew even higher into the air and began shooting fire from his eyes and flapping his wings to create a storm the likes of which the world had never seen. But the mighty little feather held firm and answered each of Thunderbird's attacks with an even greater fury. Higher and higher into the clouds the two combatants rose, fighting amid the rolling clouds and the crashing thunder, while down below, the earth shook and rain fell with a ferocity not seen since the Great Flood.

After many hours of fighting, the two magical creatures finally came together in a death grip, tumbling down to earth with such force that it shook the entire world. Raven transformed back into his original form and began to strike Thunderbird. Over and over again, Raven's blows rained down on Thunderbird. Only when the fallen spirit pleaded for mercy did Raven stop and address the tyrant.

"You are defeated," said Raven. "You shall bring no more terror to this earth. I will allow you to live, but you may only thunder on days when it is hot and humid, and your lightning may flash but not be used to destroy." Broken and defeated, Thunderbird accepted the sentence handed to him and returned to his lair on the highest peak of the mountains. From that day forward, the power of Thunderbird could still be heard, and though he still brings fear into some hearts, he seldom strikes anyone down.

Raven, Beaver and the Salmon

BEFORE THE AGE OF HUMANS, the spirits ruled the land, and all was quiet and peaceful. That is, until the Beaver woman came to alter the nature of things and bring discord to what was once harmonious. Raven was the first to notice.

Walking along the banks of the river, Raven scanned the shallows and the shores for any sign of his favourite food, salmon. Out in the open sea, the salmon swam too fast and too deep for Raven to catch, but in the rushing waters of the rivers, Raven had himself a feast every season. But one year, the salmon did not make their run.

At first, Raven did not notice anything strange as he waited on the banks of the river for the first salmon of the season to arrive. But no fish came.

They must have gotten lost or swum up another river, he thought. So Raven flapped his mighty wings and took to the air in search of a meal. Yet, each river he visited was devoid of salmon. The problem of this sudden disappearance of the salmon plagued Raven for days until he happened to fly over the home of the Beaver woman. From high in the sky, he could see how the Beaver woman had busied herself building dams at the mouth of every river. All around her home, he spied evidence of her activities in all the gnawed and felled trees. It was then that Raven spied the large home of the Beaver woman, and he knew at once that she was the cause of the salmon's disappearance.

Raven perched on a nearby rock to ponder how he would get the Beaver woman to break her dams and allow the fish to continue upriver. Luckily for Raven, the Beaver woman was rather lonely. From his rocky perch that night, Raven overheard the Beaver woman's prayers to have a child come into her life, and right then he knew what his plan must be.

Transforming himself into a little baby strapped to a piece of floating wood, Raven travelled downstream to the front door of the Beaver woman. Once within range, the baby let out a very pitiful cry that got her attention. Seeing the abandoned child greatly touched the lonesome woman's heart.

Lifting the child carefully from the water, she wrapped him in her warm furs and carried him into the safety of the lodge.

"Where do you come from, little one?" she said, looking down at the child in her arms. "The Great Spirit has heard my prayers and given me the most beautiful son. I will keep you safe and well fed, little one, until you are full grown. That I promise."

In her lodge, Raven, who was still in the form of a baby, watched as the young Beaver woman started a fire in the centre of the house. She then disappeared into a watery hole in the floor and returned with two salmon. She cut open the bellies of the fish and allowed the insides to spill onto the floor. She then placed the fish on the fire and cooked the meat until the entire lodge was filled with a most pleasant aroma.

When the fish were cooked, the Beaver woman cut off a large piece of salmon and presented it to the child. At first, Raven did not know what to make of the fired salmon, but once he had placed a piece in his mouth, he wanted more and more. He enjoyed his salmon so much that he forgot what he had come to do and fell into a deep sleep.

The next morning, the same thing occurred. The Beaver woman slipped beneath the watery hole in the floor and emerged with two more fat salmon, which she cooked on the fire and served to the happy child.

Raven spent the next week enjoying the food and comforts of the Beaver's home. He was being treated so well that he thought of staying in the form of a child and eating all the salmon he could manage. But one morning, he woke to find that the Beaver woman had changed back to her Beaver shape, and instead of the sounds and smells of a busy kitchen, he found the Beaver woman grunting about on the floor, piling sticks and bark on his plate for the morning meal. In a flash, Raven decided it was time to leave the Beaver woman's home and continue with his original plan.

As the Beaver woman busied herself about her home, Raven, in the form of the child, sat at the table and stared into the magical hole in the floor that seemed to be able to produce an unending supply of fresh salmon. He needed to get into the hole without the Beaver woman seeing. Raven patiently waited another day, and when the Beaver woman left her lodge to maintain her dams, he seized the opportunity.

Transforming back into his original form the moment the Beaver woman left the lodge, Raven went over to the hole and peered inside. Through the dark water, he could see that a tunnel had been fashioned out of sticks. Not knowing how long the tunnel was, Raven took a deep breath and slipped beneath the murky surface. For a few moments, he could not see any light ahead of him, but as he swam a little farther, a faint light appeared and continued to grow in strength as he approached.

Finally breaking the surface of the water and emerging from the other end of the tunnel, Raven could see he had entered a whole new land. Adjusting his eyes to the bright sunshine, he could see a vast expanse of land dotted with lakes and rivers, all filled with fish. He had discovered where all the rivers had been diverted, but the problem of how to return the fish and the waters to their natural state still remained.

Raven attempted to carry as many fish as he could, but he could not hold them all and kept on dropping them. Perching on a nearby rock, he looked out across the land and began to think of what he could do. Suddenly, he remembered something that his cousin Crow had taught him long ago. Ever so crafty, Crow once told Raven that if he could not fit something in his mouth, he should try rolling it into a ball to make it easier to carry. Although the lands before him were vast, Raven thought that if he could lift one end, he might be able to roll it up.

Pulling at the ground by his feet, he found that the earth lifted up off the bedrock rather easily.

In just a short time, he had rolled up all the land, lakes and rivers into a tidy package. Although it was heavy, Raven was able to pick the whole thing up in his large beak. Diving back through the magical hole in the ground, Raven emerged at the other end inside the home of the Beaver woman. He quickly darted out the front door and leapt into the sky before she returned. As he flew over the coast, most of the water and fish drained out of his neatly rolled package and fell into the empty riverbeds and lakes. By the time he reached the southern coast, Raven was tired of carrying such a heavy load and was more than happy to drop his burden into the ocean. Letting the land fall where it may, Raven created several islands along the coast, the largest of which today is called Vancouver Island. It is because of Raven that many of these islands are dotted with lakes and rivers and run thick with fish.

Origin Stories of Fire

I. Fire from Heaven

LONG BEFORE THE AGE OF HUMANS, tribes of spirit animals inhabited the world. This was a dark time, when for want of fire, the tribes suffered in the cold and were obliged to eat their meat raw. It was a difficult existence and countless innocents died in the cold darkness.

Dog was chieftain over all the tribes at that time and told the people there was nothing he could do to make their lives better. That was until he lost his daughter to a sickness she got from eating the raw flesh of a diseased animal. Her death caused the chief great pain and sorrow, and the Dog chief knew he had to use all his powers to bring light and warmth into their dark world.

Calling all the tribes together, the Dog chief issued a proclamation. "We must have fire!" he exclaimed. "We are all freezing and eating our food raw. We have all lost someone close to us because of the state we are in and something must be done. Who among you will bring us fire?"

"I have seen fire in the sky," said Raven. "I have flown high in the sky and seen that the people living in the heavens are warm and have plenty of cooked food. I say we take fire from them and bring it to earth."

Everyone quickly agreed that taking fire from the heavens was the most logical choice, but no one could agree on how to retrieve it for their use. For hours, the chiefs of the tribes discussed every possible way to steal fire from the heavens, until one scheme was finally agreed upon.

The plan was to shoot an arrow, which was attached to a very long rope, into the air, and once the arrow was securely fastened in the sky, they could climb up into the heavens and take the fire for themselves. The idea seemed simple in theory, yet it proved difficult in execution.

The Dog chief was the first to take out his bow and send an arrow into the sky. All watched as the arrow travelled higher and higher into the air, but after it reached the level of the clouds, it began to fall back to earth. The chief had not secured the arrow in sky and had failed to bring fire to his people. Other chiefs tried their hand at shooting an arrow into the sky, but all their arrows fell short of their mark and landed back on earth.

The last one to attempt the feat was the Beaver chief. Nocking his arrow, Beaver pulled back on his bow as hard as he could and released a shot that went buzzing into the sky. Everyone watched as the arrow flew higher and higher into the air, passing the clouds and finally sticking into the great canopy of the sky. Staring up at the long cord reaching from earth to the sky, the Dog chief again addressed the assembly. "Who among us will go up to the heavens and bring fire down?" he said. The Dog chief waited and waited for a reply, but no one wanted to be the first to climb up into the heavens.

"Since no one among us is willing to take on this task, I will bring the fire back," said the Dog chief. "I will slip into their realm quietly, steal the fire and carry it down in my mouth as fast as I can."

So the Dog chief began the long climb up into the heavens, while the people below watched and waited for his return.

Upon reaching the end of the rope, the Dog chief took out his knife and cut a hole in the sky. Crawling through the hole, he entered a world unlike anything he had ever seen. At first glance, the people of the heavens lived in a world similar to earth, but as the Dog chief explored this new land, he found everything to be of superior quality. The mountains in the distance were much higher, the trees were larger and filled with more life, and the water was the purest he had ever sampled. A sense of envy filled his heart as he walked about the world of the heavens. Being terribly hungry after his arduous climb, he began hunting for his next meal. But after hours of searching, the best he could find was some refuse, which he devoured in desperation. Expecting a horrible taste in his mouth, the Dog chief was instead pleased to find it full of flavour and well suited to his specific appetite. He was so filled with a desire to try other things from the land in the sky that he completely forgot the reason he had come. Instead, he was determined to remain where everything was so beautiful and tasty.

After several days of waiting for their chief's return, the tribes of the earth began to question his ultimate fate. Beaver was the first to speak, saying "It is clear that the fate of the Dog chief will not be known until someone else climbs up. I, therefore, will volunteer to go. I will retrieve the fire and also learn what has happened to our beloved chief. However, I cannot do this alone. After I have gone into the sky, I want the bravest among you to follow me. Once in the land in the sky, the people there will not know what kind of creature I am, and to satisfy their curiosity, they will most likely kill me, cut me up and eat me to see how I taste. It is while they are at the dinner table preparing to dine and distracted by their meal that I want you all to jump out and frighten them. When they run for safety, I will come back to life, steal their fire and return to earth." All agreed that Beaver's plan would succeed.

Beaver began the long climb up into the heavens, and when he got there, the people of the sky immediately set upon him. The people of the sky then killed Beaver and began preparing the evening meal. When everyone had gathered to eat, the tribes of the earth jumped out from their hiding places and frightened everyone away. Immediately, Beaver came back to life, snatched the fire of the heavens, hid it under his great tail and scurried along with the others towards the rope. Along the way, they found the Dog chief sunning himself on a rock and gnawing on a bone.

"Why must we leave this paradise, friends, when we have everything we need?" said the Dog chief.

"Your place is with the tribes of earth, and once the people of the sky find that we have stolen their fire, they will surely kill anything they do not recognize," said Beaver forcefully.

Reluctantly, the Dog chief agreed with Beaver and they immediately began their descent back to earth. But the combined weight of the raiding party was too much for the arrow to hold. The Dog chief was the first to fall to the ground, and upon impact, he transformed into the common coyote. Some of the other members of the animal tribes fell into water and remained trapped as fish, while Raven and others flew into the air as birds. Beaver landed in a wetland and remained a creature of both water and earth.

From then on, the people of earth had access to fire to keep themselves warm and to cook their food.

II. Raven and the Fire Possessed by Hags

Long before the memories of the elders of the tribes, all the fire in existence was held in the possession of two ancient, wrinkled, evil hags. While the world suffered in cold and darkness, the two bitter old ladies would neither sell nor lend nor give away any of their most prized treasure. No matter the desperation, no matter the threats, the old women were deaf to all seekers of the flame.

The lives of the people were harsh and without pleasure. To the people, fire not only meant warmth and cooked food, but it also provided light in the darkness of night and security from that which they could not see. The strongest warriors from the greatest tribes were sent to slay the hags, but the two women's magic was too strong, and the few who returned came back empty-handed. Something needed to be done to stop the suffering of the people, so a noble and distinguished chief called upon the great Raven to help them out of the dark.

Seeing the misery of the people, Raven agreed to help them, and he began working on a plan of action to wrest the fire from the hags. After much thought, Raven knew that he could not accomplish the task alone, for the women were very powerful spirits despite their aged appearance. Expecting a hard-fought struggle and possibly a fast chase, Raven called upon the fastest of the animals for their assistance. He had them stand far apart from each other but in a straight line aimed directly away from the old hags' lodge. He placed the strongest runners nearest to the home of the women and the slower runners farther away. Once everyone was in place, he told them that he would be the one to enter the hags' home, and once he had distracted them and stolen the fire, he would signal for the runners to begin their escape.

Once everyone understood the plan, Raven transformed himself into his human form and made his way towards the abode of the old women. Walking through the thick fog that surrounded the lodge,

Raven arrived at the front door and knocked loudly, shouting to the women inside that he was a weary hunter in need of a warm place to rest. The old hags yelled from inside that they did not allow strangers into their home. Raven implored the women to let him in, "Please, my ladies. I am a simple hunter with two freshly killed elk. I could give you one if you just let me in to warm my tired bones." Just then, Raven used his powerful magic to transform two large stones into the elk he had promised.

Fresh elk meat just happened to be the hags' favourite, and without hesitation, they opened the door and allowed Raven to enter.

Once inside, Raven gave the old women one of the elk and sat next to the fire while they scurried about preparing their meal. It was then, as the old women were cutting up the elk, that Raven made his move.

Pushing the women into the open belly of the dead elk, Raven quickly grabbed a brand of fire and rushed to where the first runner was waiting. Just as he handed off the brand to Mountain Lion, the old hags burst through the door of the lodge in a rage, looking for the thief who had taken their fire. Spotting Mountain Lion making off with their most prized possession, the women began to chase him. At first, Mountain Lion laughed at the old ladies, thinking that they would not be able to catch him, but within a few strides, the hags had gained a lot of ground. Although there was still a good distance between them, Mountain Lion was about to collapse from exhaustion and just managed to pass the firebrand to Bear.

Bear ran for a while, then passed the precious fire to another animal. The chase went on for some time, with the brand being passed from animal to animal, but the old hags did not tire as Raven had hoped. By the time the brand had reached the slowest of the animals—poor, squatty, little Frog—the hags were almost on top of him. It made no sense for Frog to hop any farther, as the hags were nearly upon him, so he swallowed the firebrand and jumped into a pond. Swimming to the bottom of the murky water with the coveted fire still burning in his belly, he waited for the women to tire of waiting and return to their lodge. Thinking their fire had been extinguished by the water, the old hags left with their heads hung low.

Seeing that the danger had passed, lowly Frog emerged from his watery refuge. Raven and all the other animals gathered around to see what had become of their stolen property.

"What happened to the brand of fire, Frog?" asked Raven.

Just then, Frog let out a loud "ribbit" and spit out the firebrand onto some pieces of wood. The brand, however, did not burn the dry timber but was absorbed into the fibres of the wood itself. Handing out pieces of the wood to the people, Raven said, "We have brought you what you need to make fire. Take this wood and simply rub or twirl it vigorously, and you shall be rewarded with the gift of fire."

From that moment on, the people of the coast forever had the gift of fire to keep themselves warm and secure, and to cook their food.

Raven Battles Mosquito

IN THE MARSHLANDS of a nearby valley, there once lived a giant Mosquito spirit. This enormous Mosquito was larger than any man now living, with a three-metre wingspan and a two-metre-long, needle-like sucker for a mouth. If any poor, unfortunate soul crossed the old spirit's path, the huge insect ran him through with his proboscis and drained the victim's blood. For centuries, the people of the valley had known about the Mosquito spirit, but they could do nothing to stop his reign of terror. The best warriors were summoned from the farthest lands and armed with the most expertly crafted weapons, but no one ever returned from battle victorious. With each kill, Mosquito's thirst only grew. With no end in sight to the unholy slaughter and many of their people dead, most of the tribes decided to leave the valley. Soon, only one tribe remained on its ancestral lands.

The chief of the last remaining tribe was an old and stubborn man. Not wanting to leave the lands his people had known since the dawn of time, the old chief called upon the ancient spirits to help his people in their most desperate time of need. Taking a few provisions and the tribe's fastest canoe, the old chief left his village and embarked on a journey to the home of Raven.

After three days of weary travel, the old man finally came to the land of the Raven spirit. The chief was sullen and ragged from his long journey. As he walked to the home of Raven, he sang a mournful song of his tribe's woes and beat upon his breast.

"Why have you come in sorrow to my home, noble chief of a wise people? What tribe has destroyed you?" asked Raven as the old man approached his lodge.

"I have come to seek your assistance," replied the exhausted chief. "There is a Mosquito spirit in our valley that has been devouring my people and many others for years now, and if you do not help, soon no one shall remain. I beseech you, great Raven spirit."

Falling to his knees before Raven, the old chief took one last breath and died. Raven could not refuse the elderly man's last wish, and after burying the chief's body in the ceremonial fashion of his people, Raven began to formulate a plan to rid the valley of the Mosquito spirit.

Knowing of Mosquito's hatred for smoke, Raven gathered five types of magical wood with which to make fire. He would hide these in his bosom and travel to the home of Mosquito, and once there, he would set his plan into action.

Gathering all his supplies, Raven set out on the long journey to the valley where the Mosquito spirit lived. Along the way, he sang songs honouring the sacrifice of the old chief. Raven passed through ancient forests and coastal ranges, finally reaching the valley on the third day.

When Raven entered the valley, he could smell the stench of death in the air. A dark mist covered the ground, and with each step farther into the valley, the earth became softer and softer. A slight breeze passed through the trees, clearing the mist from the ground and revealing that what Raven walked on was not soft earth, but the drained bodies of all Mosquito's victims. A shiver of fear ran through Raven as he looked upon the bodies, but he pressed on until he came to the lair of the evil Mosquito spirit.

Out of the darkness of the cave, the giant Mosquito appeared in front of Raven. "Where do you think you are going?" he said. "You will pay with your life for walking along my path."

Rather than running away in fear, Raven stood his ground and addressed Mosquito in the politest manner possible.

"My friend, I can see that you are suffering in the cold and have no fire to keep you warm. I have brought some wood so that you may warm yourself," replied Raven.

Not suspecting any deceit from his guest, Mosquito welcomed Raven into his home.

"The weather has turned colder in the last few days, and I have not had a warm meal for some time. Your gift will be most welcome," said Mosquito.

Raven entered the lair of the giant Mosquito, took out the magic wood and began to make a fire. Soon a spark finally ignited the wood, and a great blaze filled the room. But along with the flames came a thick, white smoke that blinded Mosquito. Unable to see and barely able to breathe, the evil creature fell to the ground, gasping for air. While his enemy lay prostrate on the floor of the cave, Raven seized the opportunity and put his plan into action.

Standing over the coughing Mosquito, Raven said, "No longer shall you kill the people of these lands. Although your power is great, you have abused the tribes who live in the valley, and for that you will be punished."

"You cannot harm me. I am too powerful. I am eternal," replied Mosquito.

"You may be eternal, great one, but I shall take away your power."

Then Raven raised a large stone knife and struck the head of the beast with all his might. The blow created a large hole in the head of the creature from which thousands of diminutive Mosquitoes emerged and swarmed around the lodge.

Raven had rid the world of the one giant, murderous Mosquito, but in doing so, he had created a new race of pest that even today buzzes about the heads of people and draws blood from their veins.

Since the time that Raven used smoke to defeat the giant Mosquito, its tiny brethren have been unable to tolerate the product of fires, and people have learned to protect themselves from the pest by making big, smoky blazes.

The Contest of Winds

IN TIMES LONG SINCE PAST, ancient spirits controlled the movements of the sun, the falling of the rain and the blowing of the wind. But like people, these spirits were often subject to the ebb and flow of emotions, and this sometimes led to jealousy, rage and betrayal.

In those bygone days, five brothers who lived in the south were the cause of the warm Chinook Wind that blew down from the mountains. The cold East Wind was also caused by five brothers who lived somewhere northeast of the vast mountain range. These winds had always blown over the land, but on occasion, they would rage with incredible fury.

The warm Chinook Wind would sweep through the valley, crashing into villages, tearing up trees and filling the air with dust and stones. But as bad as the five brothers of the Chinook Wind were, when the five brothers of the cold East Wind unleashed their fury on the people of the land, they would freeze everything in their path with their breath. Between the two winds, the people of the land were in a sad state of affairs and led miserable lives. To end the eternal battle between the warm Chinook Wind and the cold East Wind, the five brothers of the Chinook Wind sent a challenge to the East Wind brothers. They would compete in a series of wrestling matches to decide which wind had the right to blow across the land. The loser of each match would have his head cut off. Being very proud of their strength, the five brothers of the East Wind gladly accepted the challenge of the Chinook Wind brothers.

News of the challenge spread, and many of the spirits gathered to watch the two sets of brothers battle for control of the winds. But while the Chinook Wind brothers prepared for the match by working on their wrestling technique, the East Wind brothers were planning a deception.

While the other brothers looked on from the sidelines, the first pair faced off against one another and the first match got underway. As the East Wind brother locked arms with the Chinook Wind brother, it appeared as if the battle would swing in favour of the warmer wind. Not wanting to lose, one of the

East Wind brothers threw some water on the ground underneath the feet of the Chinook Wind brother and blew on it with his cold breath, turning it to ice. The Chinook Wind brother planted his foot directly on the ice, slipped and fell to the ground, allowing his opponent to pin him and win the match. Failing to see the treachery, the other Chinook Wind brothers accepted the defeat and allowed their brother's head to be cut off. The second Chinook Wind brother then took his place on the mat, but he suffered the same fate as the first brother, slipping on the ice, and he was beheaded as well. The East Wind brothers felt no shame in their deception and finished off all five of the Chinook Wind brothers in the same fashion. However, before the final Chinook Wind brother was defeated, Raven, who was watching the match, noticed the East Wind brothers' deception and decided to tell the family of the Chinook Wind brothers what he had seen.

Raven knew that the eldest Chinook Wind brother had a wife at home who was just about to give birth. Flying to her home, Raven told the widow the news of her husband's fate, and she vowed that day to raise her child to seek revenge on the brothers of the cold East Wind for their treachery.

With the warm Chinook Wind now wiped out, the cold East Wind brothers had complete dominance, plunging the land into permanent winter. But while the East Wind brothers wreaked havoc, the widow of the eldest Chinook Wind brother gave birth to a healthy baby boy. When he was old enough, she told him the story of his father's demise.

"Son, your father was murdered by the cold East Wind brothers," she said. "You must grow big and strong so that you might one day reclaim our family's honour and our rightful place in the natural order of things."

So the boy grew and trained hard. He became so strong that he could lift up a large redwood with one hand and toss it into the air without a second thought. Seeing that her boy had become strong enough to avenge his father's death, the Chinook Wind brother's widow let her son go into the world on his own. Travelling up rivers and through valleys, the Chinook Wind's son tore up trees and twisted off roofs along the way to the frozen lands of the cold East Wind brothers.

Arriving at the edge of the lands patrolled by the East Wind, the Chinook Wind's son felt the cold pierce his skin. The world before him lay covered in snow and ice, and he could see that the tribes were suffering. Resting at the base of a mountain for a day, the Chinook Wind's son decided to play a few tricks on the East Wind brothers as they terrorized the people.

The next morning, as the sun came up across the land, the East Wind brothers found that all the rivers and lakes had thawed during the night and the people had taken the opportunity to fish. Unable to figure out how the ice-covered lakes could have melted while the rest of the land still lay frozen, the east wind brothers blew harder across the land and covered the water in ice once more. Dismissing the occurrence as magic, the East Wind brothers retired for the night.

Upon waking the following morning, they found that the rivers and lakes had once again thawed. Just as they were about to blow their cold fury across the waters, the Chinook Wind's son appeared before the East Wind brothers.

"I am the son of the eldest brother of the Chinook Wind," said the son. "All my life, I have been told of your treachery. I have trained to become big and strong so as to challenge you to a wrestling match to once again restore order to the natural world. Do you accept my challenge?"

Shocked at the sudden turn of events, the East Wind brothers accepted the challenge and preparations began for the bout.

News of the arrival of the Chinook Wind's son spread quickly throughout the land, and the date of the wrestling match was soon announced. Although the Chinook Wind's son would fight alone against the East Wind brothers, his mother, who had made the long journey to join her son, would be standing in his corner to offer support.

Raven had also made the journey to watch the match, and before the fight began, he spoke to the Chinook Wind's widow.

"Be warned, noble lady, that the East Wind brothers do not like to lose and will most likely use the same deception that sealed your husband's fate," said Raven. He handed her a bottle of magic oil, saying, "Take this oil, but do not throw it down immediately. Even if you see that your son is almost on the ground, wait until the brothers create their ice, then throw some oil. Your son will be able to defeat all five brothers with ease."

The widow thanked Raven for his wise advice and watched as her strapping son took hold of the first East Wind brother. The battle was fierce, but the Chinook Wind's son was the stronger wrestler of the two, and just before he threw the East Wind brother to the ground, as before, one of the brothers on the sidelines threw down some water and blew his cold breath on it, turning it to ice. Seeing this, Raven yelled out to the Chinook Wind's widow, "Now! Throw your oil at his feet!"

She did as Raven commanded, throwing the oil at the East Wind brother's feet, and down to the ground he went. Having lost the match, the

Chinook Wind's son quickly chopped off the East Wind brother's head and readied himself for the next bout. The matches continued, all with the same result, until only one East Wind brother remained. The youngest of them all, seeing the fate of his brothers, refused to enter the ring to fight the son of the Chinook Wind brother.

"I will allow you to keep your head," said the Chinook Wind's son. "But you may no longer run amok, freezing the lands and the people at will. From now on, your breath may only blow lightly and bring a slight chill. I will calm my fury as well. Although I might speed through the mountaintops and melt the snow there, once I reach the valleys and the plains, I will be a warm breeze on the people's cheeks."

And from that day forward, the warm Chinook Wind would blow from the coast into the mountains and on through the plains, bringing warm relief to the chill of the cold East Wind.

The Island of
the Dead

ONE TIME, THE YOUNG CHIEF of a prosperous tribe fell
in love with a beautiful young girl. After he declared
his love for her, the young couple wed, and they
began a very happy life together. With each
passing day, they loved each other more and more,
spending their time together fishing on the water,
walking through the forest or simply relaxing in
their home. Every part of their life was spent
in happiness and celebration, until one day, the
young chief suddenly became ill and died, and his
soul departed to the land of the spirits.

For many days and nights, the girl mourned the
loss of her beloved, singing mournful songs and
refusing to leave her lodge. Their love had given her
a reason to live, and now her life seemed devoid of

all passion and exuberance. While she sank deeper and deeper into her sorrow, in the spirit world, her husband mourned as if his wife had died as well.

Surrounded by the gifts and pleasures of heaven, the young chief could not find happiness without the love of his betrothed. In the spirit world, the air was sweet, the food was divine and there was never wont for anything, but the young chief walked about with a heavy heart and depression etched deep into his face. Other spirits tried to show him the variety of pleasures that could be had, but the young chief only wanted to return to his beloved wife.

For many weeks, the two lovers passed their days in mourning, until one night, the young woman was visited in her dreams by a spirit from the land of the dead. The spirit told her that her husband was in the afterlife and had everything a man's heart could desire, but that he wanted nothing but his beloved wife. He could only find happiness if he could hold her again.

For the next three nights, she was visited by the same spirit, who told her again how her husband was suffering without her. For days, the dream of her husband's suffering weighed heavily on her mind. She wanted so much to have him back and to rescue him from his torment. Not knowing how to help her husband, she went to the village shaman and asked for his counsel on the matter. He advised the young woman that the dreams would continue as long as her husband remained in such a sorrowful mood in the afterlife, for the spirits live in happiness. However, if one of the spirits is filled with sorrow, then the heavens are thrown out of balance.

"I fear the dreams will continue and that if something is not done to appease the spirits, our village might receive a dreadful visitation from the land of the dead should we not help," said the shaman. "Together we will travel to the land of the spirits."

The next morning, the young woman and the shaman prepared a canoe for the long journey and started out across the water to the land where the spirits lived. Gliding through the calm ocean, they paddled through waters rarely visited by the living. For two days, they paddled through a great mist that surrounded them on all sides, making it difficult to navigate. But they held their course and paddled on. On the third day, the young woman began to grow frustrated and listless. She could paddle no farther and lay down in the canoe, staring into the murky water. As she looked down into the depths, at first she could see only darkness, but then strange figures began to appear. Rubbing her eyes in disbelief, she again peered down into the water and saw that the strange figures were actually ghostly spirits.

"Wise shaman, do my eyes deceive me? I am looking upon the spirits of people underneath these murky waters," she asked.

"We must be near the land of the dead, for what you see are the spirits unworthy of the pleasures of heaven. They are people who have led immoral lives and are now forced to live throughout eternity under the cold water. Do not touch the water, for if one of the spirits gets hold of you, it will grab you and pull you under, and you will never be able to break free," replied the shaman. "Prepare yourself, for we near the land of the dead. And be warned that things are not always what they seem."

A feeling of excitement and fear ran through the young woman's heart at the prospect of seeing her husband once more. Paddling through the mist, they could finally see an island off in the distance and heard the sound of drums welcoming them. Pulling up on shore just as the sun disappeared, the young woman and the shaman saw four spirits appear out of the mist.

"The girl may step foot on our shores but you, old man, must return to the land of the living. Only those who have been invited are welcome in the paradise of the dead," said one of the spirits.

The young woman got out of the canoe and bade farewell to the shaman. She was led into a great hall that was decorated with the most intricate carvings and smelled like a meadow in springtime. At the far end of the hall, she finally saw the man she had loved so much. In life he had been strong and handsome, but in the land of the spirits, he was much more beautiful. A youthful glow had been restored to his face, and all the grandeur and splendour that heaven could bestow was sewn into his garments. As soon as he saw his wife, the young chief brightened, for his heaven had been brought to him.

A grand feast was prepared, and the two lovers spent the night staring into each other's eyes while the spirits danced around them. As the light of day broke over the horizon, the revellers retired to their lodges, and the lovers went hand in hand to bed. For the first time since his journey into the land of the dead, the young chief enjoyed the blissful deep sleep awarded only to the spirits. The young woman lay cuddled safe in her husband's arms and drifted off into a peaceful slumber, but just a short time later she awoke from her sleep in a cold sweat.

Looking over to her lover for comfort, she saw not the face of the handsome man who had greeted her in the great hall, but that of a decomposing corpse. In the early morning light, she could see that his eyes had sunk deep into his bony skull, and instead of the smile she had come to love, she saw only a horrible, dirt-stained grin. Around her waist lay the bony arms and long, skeletal fingers that had caressed her naked skin. Rising out of bed, she looked down upon the rotting corpse of her husband and was suddenly overwhelmed by the stench of death. She released a horrible scream that woke her husband from his slumber. He could not see what kind of monster he had turned into and reached out for his love. Pulling back in terror, the young woman ran from the lodge screaming. The young chief, not knowing what was wrong, ran after her and called her name, but only terrible sounds came from his jaws.

Filled with terror, the young woman ran down to the water's edge looking for a means of transport back to the land of the living, but she found nothing. As her husband approached, she thought about swimming back to her homeland, but then she remembered the water spirits who wanted to hold her captive. She continued to run along the beach in a panic until she happened to stumble upon an old man and his canoe. The old man agreed to take her home, and with a push, they departed the island of the dead. Taking one look back, the young girl could see the rotting remains of her once-handsome husband on the beach, wailing to her in despair.

After three days' journey, she finally reached the land of the living and related her nightmare to family and friends. Instead of finding sympathetic ears to hear her tale of horror, the people feared for their own safety. Worried that the girl had offended the spirits of the dead, they were afraid that if the spirits were not appeased, some great misfortune might befall the tribe. For it was said that once a living person entered the land of the dead, he or she belonged to the spirit that welcomed them there. The people shamed the girl for playing with the emotions of her deceased husband. She visited the shaman, and he told her that she must return to the spirit world, for that was where she now belonged.

"Return, young one, to be with your husband, but do not look upon him during the day. Only at night will he appear as the man you fell in love with, but in daylight he will become the thing that we all fear in our nightmares. So sleep with him through the day, and celebrate your life together at night," said the shaman.

The young woman was still not convinced by the shaman's words and did not want to return to the spirit world, but her tribe feared the retribution of the spirits and sent her back to the island of the dead to be with her husband. After another long journey, she landed once more on the shore of the island at dusk and was again greeted by the same four spirits.

"Welcome back, young one. Your husband awaits in the great hall."

With great trepidation, she opened the doors to the great hall and found her husband looking as he had on the day they first met. Back in his loving arms, she spent time with her husband throughout the warm nights and slept during the days. From that time on, she never again woke in the light of day, and the couple was once again as happy as they had been in the land of the living.

After some time had passed in the land of the spirits, the young woman and her husband welcomed a beautiful son. The young chief wanted to show his new son to his mother and told his wife that he would send a spirit messenger to retrieve the grandmother so that she might travel to the island of the dead and lay eyes upon her grandchild. Once she had seen the baby, the young chief would send his son back to the land of the living with the grandmother, and then he would follow with all the other dead spirits to return to live on earth again. Because a child had been born with half a soul of the spirits and half a soul of the living, it was now possible for the two worlds to coexist on earth. The baby would bridge the gap between both worlds. Immense joy filled the young chief's heart as he awaited the arrival of his mother, and he had great hopes of one day returning to the land on which he had been raised.

The spirit messenger arrived in the home of the grandmother and told her of her son's new life in the spirit world and the arrival of a new addition to the family. Filled with a sense of longing to once again see her son, she agreed to travel to the island of the dead. Arriving on the distant shore, she was welcomed by her son and his wife. Although she would be given the opportunity to see her grandchild, she was warned that as a penance for being allowed into the spirit world, she would have to wait ten days before laying her eyes upon him.

The old lady was very curious to see her grandchild, and her curiosity grew with each passing day. By the sixth day, her curiosity had reached its peak, and unable to hold herself back, she slipped into the baby's room. She thought to herself that one little glimpse of the sleeping child would not harm anyone. Lifting the blanket that covered the child, she peered into the crib and saw the little angel sleeping quietly. But her penance was not yet completed, and as she gazed at the child, it died before her eyes.

The grandmother's actions greatly displeased the spirits, and from that day on, the world of the dead and the world of the living were never again allowed to come into contact. The grandmother returned to the land of the living in shame, and the young chief and his wife remained behind on the island of the dead and were never heard from again.

The Giant

LONG AGO, THE BOYS of a certain village liked to play at the edge of a dark forest. Their parents would always tell them to stay away from the woods, for many unknown creatures lurked under its dark canopy, and many boys had disappeared, never to return. But boys being boys, they did the exact opposite of what their parents told them and could be found most days playing along the edge of the woods.

As the children were playing, the smallest of the bunch pulled out a knife. The other children stopped playing and stared at the boy. "Can I see it?" asked one of the boys.

"No, I can't let anyone play with it," said the boy with the knife. "It is my father's knife, and it is really important to him. My mother said that

I wasn't to let anyone touch it because someone might get hurt."

"Don't be such a baby. Let me see the knife. I promise I will give it right back," said another boy.

"No, I promised my parents," said the boy with the knife.

Angry over their rejection, the other boys refused the play with the boy with the knife. They teased him and called him names, finally turning away and leaving him at the edge of the forest all by himself.

Alone near the woods with his knife, the boy wandered into the forest looking for a good piece of wood to carve. But he had barely taken two steps into the trees when he saw a large figure in the shadows. Running out of the forest in terror, he yelled to the other boys, "Hey! I saw something or someone in the woods!"

The other children simply ignored his cries and continued playing their games. "You're a liar. You just want someone to play with," said one of the boys.

"I swear, I'm not lying," pleaded the boy. "Look, there it is again. The shadow is bigger than any of our fathers. It is watching us. I can hear it breathing."

The boys continued to ignore him, thinking that he was just playing a trick on them. "Just because you say something doesn't mean we will listen to you. Go. Don't bother us any more," said another boy, turning his back.

But just as he finished speaking, the shadowy figure in the forest moved into the light. "It's coming!" screamed the boy with the knife.

Only when the other boys heard his scream did they finally turn around and see that he was not lying. What had emerged from the forest was no man. It stood as high as a grizzly bear on two legs and was covered in just about as much hair as a grizzly. Its cold, black eyes were deeply set in its skull, and strangest of all was that he carried a large basket on his back. The children would have run away, but fear gripped their little bodies as the monster moved towards them.

The giant reached out his dirty paw, grabbed the boy with the knife and threw him into the basket. The giant then lumbered over to the other boys, grabbing them one by one and throwing them on top of the boy with the knife. He then walked back into the darkness of the forest while the children cried and tried to look through the cracks in the basket, hoping to see the direction in which they were headed.

The boy with the knife was at the bottom of the basket and could not easily move. He struggled for a few moments to free his knife, and after more struggling, he was able to cut a hole in the basket just big enough for him to fit through. Luckily, the screams of the other boys distracted the giant, and he failed to notice that one of the boys had escaped. Running back through the forest, the boy made his way back to the village and alerted everyone to what had happened. "Help! Help!" he cried. "A giant has taken all the boys!"

The boy quickly recounted the story of the shadowy giant in the forest. Once he had finished his tale, the men of the village gathered their weapons and asked the boy to lead them to where the giant had taken the children.

Fearing that evil spirits had taken their boys, the people called upon Raven for his help, but their calls went unanswered. No doubt Raven was involved in some other mischief or simply could not be bothered to come to their assistance.

So the men travelled through the forests with the boy leading them up to the point where he had stumbled out of the basket. From there, the trail was easy to follow as the giant cut a large path through the woods, leaving behind his massive footprints and a bunch of broken bushes. A short while later, the trail ended abruptly in front of a large cave.

Afraid of what they might find inside, the men of the village peered into the darkness of the cave and could see the figure of a large man hanging children upside down by their feet. They could also see that the giant was not alone and that he had a family of his own.

"Leave them alone!" cried one of the men from the village. "What are you going to do with our children?"

"Why, we are going to cook your children and eat them, of course," answered the giant in a loud, booming voice.

"You cannot eat our children! Return them to us. We wish to take them back to our village," said one of the men.

Stepping out into the light of day, the giant towered over the men of the village. They could see his horrible sunken eyes, hair-covered face, gnarled teeth and incredible size. They knew their tiny weapons would be useless against such a formidable opponent. Not knowing what to do, one of the men pleaded with the giant, "Please, kind sir, do not cook and eat our children."

Looking down upon the faces of the men surrounding him, the giant noticed for the first time how clean and handsome they were. "Why are your faces not like my own? Yours are smooth and without hair, while I am rough and ugly."

Using the giant's moment of distraction, the father of the boy with the knife thought quickly and said, "Well, you can have a face like ours, and we know just how to do it. Lie down here on this rock and close your eyes. We will bring a sharpened stone and clean your face so that it is smooth and handsome like ours."

Not sensing any deception, the giant gladly lay down on the rock and closed his eyes. "How long will this take? I am hungry. And so is my family," said the giant.

"Just two days, but when it is completed, you will look just like us, and your wife will love you more," said the father of the boy with the knife.

The giant closed his eyes tightly, and the men of the village took a sharp rock and brought it down hard on his head, killing the giant instantly.

Seeing her husband lying on the floor with a rock in his head, the giant's wife asked how long it would take before her husband would emerge looking different. "Oh, about two days," said one of the men.

While the wife was occupied watching her husband, the men of the village untied the children and ran back to the village. After the incident with the giant, the children never again played near the forest, and the other boys never teased the little one with the knife.

Raven and the Two-Headed Serpent

―――――〜〜〜〜〜〜〜―――――

It HAPPENED ONE EVENING that Raven was sitting at home by the fire with his wife, talking about nothing in particular. It was a quiet night, and all was peaceful in the forest. Suddenly they heard a horrendous noise in the distance. Raven and his wife grew fearful and wondered what could have made such a spine-chilling sound.

As the noise grew louder and louder and the ground began to shake, Raven knew immediately what was causing all the commotion. It was the two-headed serpent, Senotlke, and he was on a rampage. Raven knew that the monster would not stop its destruction and that it would have to be killed.

Raven turned to his wife and said, "I will go and dispose of this monster. He has plagued our land for too long. I will be away for four years. Do not sing sorrowful songs in my honour, for I will return."

After preparing his supplies, Raven departed from his home at the break of dawn, saying good-bye and embracing his wife one last time before leaving. Along with food, he took his fire-starting tool and his trusted stone knife.

Tracking the serpent proved easy, as the beast left a large swath of destruction in its wake. After following the creature's path for several days, Raven finally saw the serpent monster. He was astounded at the actual size of the beast as it lay on the ground, soaking in the sunshine. Each of the giant's great heads was the size of a full-grown grizzly bear, and its body was as thick and long as the largest tree in the forest. But what shook Raven the most was the size of the serpent's fangs. They looked like his mother's sewing needles, but they were as long as the height of an average man and most likely held enough poison to kill a thousand elk. In fact, all around him, Raven saw the remains of elk, deer, bears and many more animals strewn about the forest. Senotlke's fury had been so great that many of the carcasses had not even been feasted upon. Raven knew that he was faced with a creature that killed more for pleasure than necessity.

For months, Raven stalked the beast, looking for any sort of weakness he might use to slay the monster. However, the more closely he watched the serpent, the more scared Raven became. He would watch as the serpent moved through the forest, indiscriminately killing every living thing that crossed its path. Raven knew he could not defeat Senotlke without some kind of magical power or help. Searching through the forest, he found a special herb that he rubbed on himself. When he awoke the next morning, Raven found that he was no longer afraid of the two-headed serpent and he possessed the strength of ten men. Gathering up some spruce trees, he fashioned two large spears and a swift canoe to use in his attack on the monster. Now Raven just had to wait for the right moment to strike.

Raven watched the serpent for ten days, taking note of its every move. He watched the beast as it slept and watched as it fed. For those ten days Raven did not sleep. He concluded after watching the serpent for so long that the best time to strike would be after a meal when it went into a lake to bathe.

Following the creature one day, he watched as it ate ten goats and slithered into the lake. When the giant serpent fell asleep in the water, Raven set out in his canoe and used his giant spruce spears to pierce each head, killing the snake instantly. But no sooner had he killed Senotlke than he himself fell down dead. Remaining dead for ten days, Raven suddenly came back to life and looked about him for the dead serpent. But instead of finding the enormous body of the creature, he found only bones and its tongues. Raven guessed that he had died because he had been so close to the poisonous breath of the beast but had been spared true death because of the magic herb still on his skin. As proof of his heroics, Raven took the lower jaws and the tongues of the serpent, hanging them around his neck as decorations. It had been exactly four years since he had left his home to kill the two-headed snake.

Raven began the long journey back to his wife, and after several days, he came upon a village. A young lad from the village noticed the stranger from afar and called out that someone was approaching. Raven was hungry and wanted to ask for shelter for a few days before again moving on. But as soon as the villagers came close to Raven, they all suddenly fell to the ground dead because of the evil magic emanating from the jaws and tongues of the serpent.

"What have I done?" thought Raven.

Making a fire, he threw the magic herb into the flames, and the resulting smoke spread over the people, waking them from the dead. Grateful to the stranger for saving their lives, the villagers gave him food and shelter for a day before he continued towards his home.

As Raven walked on, though, everyone he encountered died the moment they came near him, and he was forced to use the magic herb to revive them. So he decided to place the jaws and tongues in goatskins that had been soaked in the magic herb. He hoped he would not kill any more people, but despite his precautions, whomever he met fell down dead. Raven cried at his fate for killing the serpent and lamented the fate of his wife as he came upon his own land.

When he arrived at his village, not only did all his people die in front of him, but Raven also found that his wife had been murdered by a neighbouring tribe. Angry at the injustice, he got into his canoe and paddled to the land of the rival tribe. When he showed them the jaws and tongues of the two-headed serpent, they all died. Raven returned to his home, burned more of the magic herb, and his people came back to life. For his bravery and to cele-brate his new powers, a ten-day feast was thrown to commemorate the heroism of Raven.

Raven and the Humble Swallow

IT SO HAPPENED that Raven and Swallow lived in the same village. When the winter winds returned to their home in the mountains and the herring returned to the seas, Raven and Swallow both went fishing.

All day, Raven caught many fish, but Swallow was having terrible luck. Often, fellow fishermen will come to the aid of one another in times of need, but selfish Raven only helped himself. Swallow returned to his home and told his wife that he had not caught even one fish. Swallow's children were very hungry and cried all day and night. The children became so hungry that they went around the village looking for food, eventually coming to the house of Raven.

The children could smell the herring he had caught cooking over the fire and wanted to see the feast for themselves. Looking through the knot-holes in the wall, they could see Raven preparing his day's catch. Noticing that he had visitors, Raven began mocking the children by showing them the fish and eating right in front of them. One of the children cried out, "Scoundrel!" and hearing that, Raven poked their eyes with a stick through the holes.

Running back home, the children showed their father their injuries, and he became very angry with his neighbour. Wanting to show Raven that he was a good provider for his family, Swallow took up his bow and arrows and went into the forest to hunt. After several hours, he wandered into the land of the Wolves, but he continued to hunt, wanting to prove he was better than Raven despite the danger.

After some time, he came across a large herd of elk and killed two bucks. As he was skinning them, a pack of Wolves passed by and asked Swallow, "How did you kill those elk, stranger?" He answered, "I believe it was you who killed them, great Wolf. I found them here dead. You must have forgotten your kill."

Then the pack leader replied, "Yes, I think you are right. You may keep the elk for we have already eaten our fill today. How, might I ask, are you going to get these large elk home?"

"I was going to carry them as best I could," said Swallow. "Do you want to help?"

"Yes, we can help. Place the meat on your back," replied Wolf.

"But I cannot, for you see, I am just a tiny bird and not very strong," said Swallow.

"Do not worry, little one. Just place the elk on your back and we shall do the rest," replied the Wolf leader.

So Swallow painfully lifted the meat and placed it on his back, almost collapsing from the weight. Just as he was about to fall to the ground, the pack leader said, "Light!" and suddenly Swallow was able to lift the elk with no effort at all.

Returning home, he presented his wife with the meat, and she immediately started a fire for the feast. As his wife prepared the meal, Swallow went around his home and plugged up all the holes and joints in his house. But despite his efforts, Raven was still able to smell the tasty meat and fat as it roasted over the fire.

Raven went right to Swallow's house. "What are you roasting? I know you did not catch anything, for you are a terrible hunter," said Raven mockingly.

But Swallow simply ignored Raven's words. Then Raven returned home and got some of the herring he had caught and brought the fish to Swallow's house.

"I have brought you some herring. Please tell me what you are roasting," pleaded Raven. But his words fell on deaf ears, and Raven had to return home.

Angry at being ignored, Raven gulped down the last of the herring and went into the forest to try his luck in the hunt. "If Swallow can kill something so tasty, I will bring back something far better," Raven said to himself.

Wandering through the forest for several hours, Raven finally came upon a herd of elk and killed two large bucks. While he was skinning the elk, the same Wolf tribe that helped Swallow came upon Raven.

"How did you kill those elk?" asked the pack leader.

"What do you think?" cried Raven proudly. "I killed them myself. I am Raven, and I don't need anyone's help."

"Then how will you carry the meat home?" asked the Wolf.

"Stupid Wolf, I will easily put them on my back and take them home," said Raven, insulting the Wolves.

Raven then picked up the elk and threw them on his back. Dragging them back to the village with great trouble, he threw the elk onto the ground in front of Swallow's house and called out, "Come and see, Swallow, for I am a better hunter than you are. I have two large elk here for roasting, and I did not need the help of those stupid Wolves."

Opening the door, Swallow looked down onto the ground behind where a very proud Raven stood. "I see no elk meat, only rotten flesh," said Swallow.

Raven then turned around to see that his meat was covered with maggots.

"You certainly are a great hunter, Raven," said Swallow, laughing. "But when in another land, make sure to pay respect to those you visit."

Disheartened, Raven returned home, but Swallow continued to laugh through the night while feasting on his tasty elk.

Hungry Raven Gets Some Berries

ONCE, TWO WOMEN wanted to take a box of berries to their sister in a distant village. Their friends were worried about them travelling the long distance by themselves and called upon Raven to escort them. Raven, seeing the large box of berries, agreed to escort the women, and the next day, they prepared the canoe and set off for the village. The women sat up front and paddled, while Raven sat at the back and steered.

On the way, Raven could not help but stare at the box of berries, and after several hours in the canoe, he began to get very hungry. However, he knew that the treat was not meant for him, so he devised a plan to trick the women and get the berries all to himself.

When they had gone a little farther downstream, the air became thick with fog. Raven called out to the women. "Oh no, I can see with my magical vision that far off, a canoe is approaching," he said. "I can see that they are enemies from a very war-like tribe and want to kill us or make us slaves. You must stare straight ahead and paddle as fast as you can. Do as I say, and you will survive. Fail, and you shall perish."

The women became terrified at the prospect of dying at the hands of enemy warriors and did exactly what Raven instructed. They paddled and paddled until they finally reached land.

"You must go and hide yourselves in the forest. I will remain behind and disguise the canoe. Run! Run now or die!" cried Raven.

Fearing the worst, the women were in such a panic that they completely forgot about their box of berries in the canoe. As they ran into the woods, Raven called out, "You there! Beware! Come and attack, and I shall kill you."

Between his shouts, Raven was eating the berries, and soon they were all gone. In order to continue with the deception, Raven poured the red berry juice all over himself, broke off a piece of the canoe and smashed the box that had contained the berries. Lying down next to the faked battle scene, Raven called out to the women to return.

"It is safe, ladies. I have defeated the warriors, but I am afraid your possessions took a beating."

When the women returned, they saw Raven lying on the ground covered in dirt and berry juice. They attempted to tend to his wounds as a gift for protecting them, but he stopped them for fear that they would discover his deception. Everyone got back into the canoe and returned to the village. Raven thought he had fooled everyone, but he had eaten so many berries that he was very ill for several days afterwards.

Raven's Bad Advice

IN THE OLDEN DAYS, the Great Spirit held a council to decide where to place the genitals on the new human race. Raven called out to the council to have them put on the forehead, but the wise Heron said, "No, they shall be placed between the legs, where they cannot be seen." And it was thus adopted.

Raven Creates Mountains

RAVEN MADE HIS HOME on a certain stretch of coast where he enjoyed his favourite pastime of collecting and eating delicious fish and other tasty morsels that washed up on the beach. On a day like any other, at the crack of dawn, Raven went down to the beach to fetch his breakfast but found that all the fish and creatures of the sea had disappeared. Unable to understand why there were no fish, he decided to wait until the next day, when he would wake earlier to catch his morning meal.

Waking before the light of day hit the water, Raven walked down to the beach and found that the beach was once again empty. "Thieves must be raiding my beach," thought Raven, and he became very angry. He decided to wake up even earlier the next day, but again he found that someone had absconded with his food. Wanting to get to the bottom of the thievery, Raven hid in some bushes and waited up all night. Finally, he was able to see the thief, and by the faint light of the moon, he caught Wolf in the act. "I will get revenge on this Wolf," thought Raven.

Raven called out to Wolf, "Next time you come down to the beach, friend, you must come by my house and we will share a meal."

Wolf agreed happily, and the next morning, he came to Raven's house and entered his home.

Lying down by the fire, Wolf fell into a comfortable sleep. Meanwhile, Raven took out his spear, sharpened the edge and stood over Wolf as he slept. "You shall no longer steal from me," he said and plunged the spear into Wolf's head, killing him instantly. Raven then buried Wolf's body and went out to collect his breakfast on his beach.

The next day, two members of the Wolf tribe came by Raven's home and enquired about their friend's whereabouts. "Have you seen our pack leader, kind Raven?" they asked.

"Why no, I haven't," replied Raven. "I have been sick for some time, and I have not left the comfort of my home." The two Wolves thanked him for his time and left.

But a few days later, others from the Wolf tribe showed up on Raven's stretch of beach looking for their chief. "I am sorry, friends, but I have not seen your chief. I have been ill and have been lying on the floor of my lodge in front of the fire," said Raven.

Several days later, more Wolves showed up at Raven's home and asked about the missing Wolf chief. "We have heard whispers on the wind that our chief was killed along this stretch of the coast near your home," said one of the Wolves.

"Oh, really. That is certainly perplexing. I have been laid out here with sickness, but as soon as I recover, I will look for him," said Raven.

It was then that yet more Wolves showed up looking for their chief, refusing to leave Raven's stretch of coast until they knew the fate of their leader. For two days, the wolves remained, and their presence began to annoy Raven. He formed a plan to get rid of the Wolves, for Raven always has a scheme.

Taking up a comb and a bladder of fish oil, he hid them beneath his feathers and asked all the Wolves to gather in a circle. Raven began dancing about in the circle and singing a mournful song to the spirits, but after the first few verses, he changed the song and began to sing, "It is I who killed the chief of the Wolves! It is I who killed the chief of the Wolves! Ka-ka-ka!" Hearing that, the Wolves began to growl and show their fangs, ready for a fight to the death. Raven jumped out of the circle, and the Wolves took after him at top speed.

Knowing that he could not out run the speedy Wolf tribe, Raven took the comb from beneath his feathers and thrust it into the ground. He called out, "Rise up, mountain!" and suddenly a mountain sprang up in front of the Wolves, blocking their path.

But the Wolves were able to run around the mountain, so Raven thrust the comb into the ground again and called out, "Rise up, mountain!" and another mountain blocked the Wolves' path.

But again the Wolves sprinted around the mountain and caught up to Raven.

Raven knew that Wolves did not like water, so he took out the bladder of fish oil and poured the oil on the ground behind him. The oil transformed into a large lake, and the Wolves could not get around it easily. So Raven ran ahead and made more mountains and lakes along the coast. That is why there are so many mountains and lakes along the coast to this very day.

Raven Spears
a Shark

ONE MORNING, RAVEN AWOKE at first light and prepared his canoe for a full day of fishing. He was hoping to catch a few of his favourite fish: halibut, red snapper and salmon. The ocean was very calm that morning, and that usually meant a good day of fishing, so Raven was very happy and excited. After paddling out to sea, he baited his lines and was just about to put them into the water when he saw a shark swim right underneath his canoe, driving away all the fish.

Raven was hungry and he became very angry at the shark. He began yelling at it from above the water, but the shark could not hear him and continued to swim about. So Raven paddled back to the shore and fetched his spear so he could catch the shark the next time he went fishing.

The next morning, at the break of dawn, Raven prepared his canoe and made sure that he had his trusted spear by his side in case the shark reappeared. Sure enough, as soon as Raven dropped his baited lines in the water, there was the shark, right beneath the canoe.

Fury swept through Raven's blood as the shark scared away another meal, but this time Raven would get his revenge. Taking up his spear, he waited patiently, poised over the water and ready to strike. When the shark came closer to the canoe, Raven lashed out and speared the shark in the back. Raven tried to hold onto the spear, but even injured, the shark was too powerful, and it disappeared deep into the ocean.

After the shark disappeared, Raven continued to fish and finally caught his breakfast. Heading home, he decided that he would go out the next day and search along the beach to see if the body of the shark had washed up on the shore.

The next morning, after eating a breakfast of salmon and dried clams, Raven set out along the beach to look for the shark's body, but after several hours, he could not find any sign of the injured or dead shark. However, just when he was about to give up and return to his lodge, he came across a village he had never encountered before. Still some distance outside the village, he could hear the rhythmic song of a shaman in one of the houses.

Raven called out to the people in the house, but no one could hear him over the singing. Finally, after calling three more times, a woman inside heard him and sent a messenger slave to see what he wanted.

The messenger ran outside and said to Raven, "The lady of our village is sick. Our shaman has been trying to heal her, but with each passing moment, her condition becomes worse. If nothing is done, she will surely die. Can you please help us, stranger?"

Raven agreed to help if he could, and the slave led him into the lodge of the sick woman.

Through the faint light pouring down from a hole in the roof, Raven could see his spear sticking out of the woman's back, and he knew instantly that he was in the village of the Shark tribe. A group of Shark people stood around the woman, looking for the thing that had caused her sudden sickness, but because of their unique eyes, which enable them to see in the oceans, the Shark people were blind to the spear sticking out of the woman's back. They thought her illness was caused by a parasite that was crawling around underneath her skin.

Raven walked up to the woman and laid his hands upon her head. "Fear not, noble Shark. I am a healer, and I shall make the pain and sickness go away," he said.

Raven began to chant and wave his arms over the sick Shark woman. One of the Shark people then said to Raven, "If you heal her, then she will give you one of her daughters to marry. They are the most beautiful women in our village, and her daughter will make you a happy man."

"If you promise me two of her beautiful daughters to marry, then I will heal her now," said Raven, greedily taking advantage of the Shark people.

The Shark tribe agreed to Raven's request, so he placed his hands on the spear and pulled it out of the woman's back. Before any of the Shark people could see what Raven had removed, he tossed the spear out of the house and into the ocean.

The sick Shark woman sat up immediately and thanked Raven for his help. "I feel that my sickness has been cast out. For your kindness, you will receive my two beautiful daughters' hands in marriage."

Raven married the two Shark girls and took them home. But because of the Shark women's rough skin, Raven wore down his penis, and it eventually broke off. So Raven threw his penis down the coast, and it landed near Barkley Sound at a place that is now called Knob Point.

Raven Holds the Sun

IT HAPPENED ONE DAY that the people began teasing Raven, saying that he could not reach the sun. At this, Raven cried out, "You forget to whom you are speaking. I have been to visit the spirit of the Sun before and, in fact, he is my father."

Raven had lied, but he wanted to prove to the people that he was an important spirit. But then the people teased him even more and asked him to prove that he was the offspring of the Sun spirit. "But how will you get up into the sky? It is far too long a journey to undertake, and your wings will surely tire before you reach the home of the Sun," said one of the people.

"I will show you," said Raven.

So Raven went to see his cousin Crow and borrowed his bow and arrows. Taking the bow and arrows to a clearing, Raven aimed an arrow towards the sky and released the string. Up the arrow flew until it stuck in the sky. Raven then shot arrow after arrow into the air until a chain had formed that reached from the sky down to the earth. Raven said goodbye to the people and began his long climb up to the home of the Sun. For several hours, he climbed the chain of arrows and, finally, almost collapsed from exhaustion. Taking a magic herb from beneath his cloak, he placed the leaf under his tongue and suddenly had the strength of ten men. With renewed energy, Raven was able to reach the end of the arrow chain and cut a hole in the sky with his knife. Crawling through the opening he had made, Raven reached the house of the Sun and called out, "Is anyone home? I have come a long way and seek council with the Sun."

Someone inside must have heard him because a slave came running out. When the slave saw Raven at the door, he ran back inside to his master and said, "You have a visitor from earth outside."

The Sun spirit was extremely happy to have a visitor and told his slave to invite Raven inside. Raven entered the house and sat down by the fire and spoke to the Sun, "I have come from earth to see you. I am your son."

The Sun spirit sat by the fire in an expertly carved chair. He was a very old spirit. All his hair had turned white, and because of his age, some of his teeth had fallen out.

"I do not recall having a son on earth, but my memory is not very good of late. If you say you are my relative, then I have no reason not to believe you," said the Sun. "In fact, I am extremely glad that you have arrived. It is getting too hard for me to carry the sun every day because I am old and weak. Now that you are here, you shall carry my burden."

The Sun spirit then told Raven to bathe and get a good night's rest, for in the morning, he would have to hold the sun throughout the day. The next morning, the Sun spirit woke Raven while darkness still covered the land and explained to him the rules for holding the light in the sky.

"You must not walk too quickly, for you could burn the earth below and cause great havoc. This is not a game, and you must be patient," said the Sun. Raven half-heartedly agreed to the old spirit's rules, and the Sun placed the light in his hands. Everything started off smoothly as Raven walked slowly across the sky, and he could see down below that the light spread across the earth.

The Sun spirit watched from his home, making sure that Raven followed his instructions to the letter. But around the middle of the afternoon, clouds began to gather in the sky, blocking Raven's path.

Never a patient creature, Raven pushed the clouds aside and ran quickly past them. As Raven was running, he tripped and dropped the sun down the hole he had cut in the sky. The sky caught on fire, and the oceans began to boil away. When the Sun spirit saw this, he ran over to the hole, reached down and picked up the sun before it hit the earth below and killed every living creature. The Sun spirit returned and was very angry at Raven. "You cannot be my son. My offspring would not be so impatient and stupid. Leave this world and return to earth." Then the Sun grabbed Raven by his beak and threw him down from the sky.

Raven fell back down to his village, and the people said, "Raven, you have returned so quickly. What happened?"

"Well, it turns out that not all fathers are proud of their sons," explained Raven.

Raven Causes Several Problems

IT HAPPENED ONE DAY that a very powerful chief heard a rumour that his wife had been cheating on him. When he discovered this, he became very angry and confronted his wife.

"Why have you cheated on me and brought me great dishonour in front of our people?" asked the chief. His wife denied ever having an affair, but he did not believe her.

Raven happened to overhear the couple's quarrels and spied on the wife while the chief was away. He saw that whenever the chief left the village, the wife's lover would sneak into her lodge and would stay there for a couple of hours. Wanting to teach the woman a lesson for breaking the covenant of marriage, Raven devised a plan.

When the chief's wife went down to the river to fetch water, he used his magic to make her thirsty, then he transformed himself into a tiny pine needle and jumped into the woman's pitcher. When she took a drink, Raven settled in her stomach and transformed into a human baby. The months passed, and the wife noticed that she was pregnant. Thinking it to be the child of her lover, she feared what her husband might do, so she left her husband's village to live with her lover.

It came time for the woman to give birth, and on that day, a beautiful baby boy was born. But the next day, the woman noticed that something was different about this baby, for in just two days, the child had grown to the size of a toddler and kept crying for food. The villagers caught several fish and gave them to the boy, but he wanted more. If he was not fed, the child cried louder and louder, so the villagers brought the boy more fish. He gobbled them up greedily and cried for more. It wasn't long before the child had eaten everything in the house, and eventually the village had no food, either. That is when the boy spoke to his mother, "I am Raven and I have punished you for dishonouring your husband, the chief."

Because the woman had angered the spirits, the people of the village abandoned their homes and left her behind as punishment. She died some time later of loneliness and hunger. Raven went into the forest to look for more food.

~~~~~~

As Raven wandered through the forest, he met Mink, and they decided to become friends.

"Would you like to wander the earth with me?" asked Raven.

Mink agreed, and they headed towards the coast. While they were wandering along the coast, the new friends encountered Whale. Raven called Whale closer to the shore and asked, "Excuse me, Whale. We would like you to carry us through the water to a distant island. Will you take us?"

"Certainly. Please climb into my mouth, and we will begin the long journey together," replied Whale.

So Raven and Mink climbed into Whale's mouth, and the great beast dove beneath the water. After several hours of travel, Raven became hungry, but he knew he could get no food from the inside of Whale's mouth. So Raven devised a plan.

He reached out and pinched Mink so hard that it made him cry. Mink's crying eventually caught the attention of Whale, and he asked his two passengers what all the tears were about. Raven responded,

"Well, kind sir, my friend here is hungry, and we have nothing to eat with us." Then Whale said, "Well, little ones, you may cut a piece of meat from me to satisfy your hunger."

So Raven and Mink cut out a piece of meat and blubber from Whale and ate it up. Then a short while later, Raven became hungry again, so he pinched Mink even harder. Hearing Mink's cries once more, Whale told them that they could cut out another piece of meat. "Take as much as you desire, but I must ask that you do not cut my throat, for if you do, I will die," said Whale.

No sooner had Whale finished his sentence than Raven took out his knife and slit Whale's throat, killing him instantly.

Whale's body floated about for months, and Raven and Mink continued to eat away at the carcass from the inside until one day it washed up on shore.

Two fishermen, seeing Whale on the beach, began to cut the carcass open, and they noticed that something had been eating it from the inside. When they finally came to the stomach and cut it open, Raven and Mink jumped out and ran off with their bellies full.

Raven and Mink decided to separate. Mink wanted to return home, while Raven wanted to continue to explore the world. One day, Raven happened upon a village that was having a feast. From afar, he saw that they had prepared enough food for the entire village. Raven, being a slave to his desires, wanted everything they had and thought up a plan to get it.

Raven transformed into an old man and went into the forest to relieve himself. Once he had relieved himself all around the village, he spoke to his excrements, "I command you to yell when I give the word."

So Raven, still disguised as the old man, limped into the village and began shouting, "The village is surrounded! Your enemies are coming! Your enemies will kill you!" Raven then signalled to his excrements, and they began a war-like cry that sounded like hundreds of warriors approaching. Fearing for their lives, the villagers fled into the forest. Raven transformed back into his normal self and devoured the people's feast, leaving nothing behind. The villagers only discovered the trick when they ran into the forest and stepped in Raven's excrements. When they returned, they saw that they had been the victims of deception.

Tired of walking, Raven pushed off the land and flew high into the sky. While soaring through the air, Raven noticed two fishermen out on the ocean. He was getting hungry from flying for so long and decided to have a little fun with the fishermen.

Diving into the water, Raven swam under the boat and gobbled up all the bait off the men's hooks. The fishermen thought they had caught something, but when they reeled in their lines, they found that all their bait had been eaten. Thinking that a shark had devoured the bait, they decided to catch it and roast it for dinner. So they baited their hooks with larger pieces of fish and put their lines back into the water.

Raven was waiting below and ate all the meat off the hooks. But in his haste to get all the food, Raven failed to notice that his beak had gotten caught on one of the hooks, and he began to panic.

One of the fishermen, thinking he had caught the shark, began pulling hard on his line. Raven could not fight the strength of the fisherman and found himself being pulled up to the surface. In a last-ditch effort not to get caught, Raven placed his feet against the bottom of the canoe and pulled back as hard as he could. But the fisherman pulled just as hard, and Raven's beak broke off.

The fisherman reeled in his catch. Holding up Raven's broken beak, he asked his friend, "Do you know what this is?"

"No, but let us take it back to the village and ask the old wise man," said the other fisherman.

Meanwhile, Raven had transformed into an old man and went into the forest to fetch a fake nose. Grabbing a suitable piece of wood, he constructed an artificial nose and walked into the village of the two fishermen. Raven, still in the form of an old man, asked the first person he saw, "I hear that two fishermen caught a strange fish in the sea. Can you tell me where they are?"

The man pointed to the lodge of one of the fishermen, and Raven shuffled over to the house. He knocked on the door, and when the fisherman answered, Raven asked if he could see his strange catch. The fisherman obliged the old man and pointed to the fire, where Raven's beak had been hung to dry.

When the fisherman turned around for a moment, Raven grabbed his beak and put it back on his face. He then transformed back into his Raven form and flew out of the chimney.

That day, Raven learned that some things are better left untouched, for tasty morsels can disguise hidden dangers.

ESCHIA
BOOKS

Here are more titles from
ESCHIA BOOKS...

MYTH OF THE BARRENS
by Bren Kolson
Living on the Barren Lands of northern Canada in winter is a unique experience most Canadians will never know. Bren Kolson, a young Métis woman, spends eight months over two years with a Chipewyan elder and a white man on the Barren Lands. The extreme cold and isolation challenges her while she learns to survive life above the treeline where few people dare to live. Kolson's compelling narrative vividly describes hunting trips to outpost camps, living in a caribou-skin tent and a log cabin, an experience with a wolverine and the two dog-team trips from the Barren Lands to Fort Reliance on the eastern arm of Great Slave Lake. *Myth of the Barrens* is a frank account of how one woman learned to live off the land with no human contact for days on end while her two companions hunted and trapped. She revisited her Aboriginal roots and the experience awakened a deep spirituality within her not taught by words in a structured religion. Living on the land was a journey of renewal of her culture and heritage, filled with new experiences of self-discovery. The accompanying photographs highlight the beauty of the land and take us back to a time when living off the land was the way of life for Aboriginal Canadians.
$14.95 • ISBN: 978-0-9810942-4-3 • 5.25" x 8.25" • 320 pages

WATISHKA WARRIORS
by Daniel Auger
After living in the city for years, Sandy Lafonde returns to her childhood home at Watishka Lake First Nation to care for her ailing aunt. Little has changed since she left—a young teen has just committed suicide, a local gang menaces the area, the community is splintered and dysfunctional, and the youth are left restless and frustrated. Sandy feels the need to do something for her community, so she proposes to start a junior hockey team. She initially meets resistance, first from the band council and then from the team itself, who can barely stop fighting long enough to play hockey. Drawing on her own past, Sandy steps in as coach and tries to rein in the star player, hot-headed Sheldon Lambert, a 15-year-old hockey prodigy who just can't seem to stay out of trouble. Sandy struggles to keep the team and the community together despite crippling odds and the ever-present gang lurking in the background. And Sheldon faces decisions that could affect the fate of the team, and his own life.
$14.95 • ISBN: 978-0-9810942-2-9 • 5.25" x 8.25" • 168 pages

Available from your local bookstore or by contacting the distributor,
Lone Pine Publishing
1-800-661-9017
www.lonepinepublishing.com